The Liturgy of Marriage

BUILDING YOUR RELATIONSHIP
WITH THE *RITE* STUFF

Timothy A. Heck, Ph.D.

Cradle Press
P.O. Box 8401
ST. LOUIS, MO 63132

Nihil Obstat: Most Reverend Timothy Doherty
Diocese of Lafayette, Indiana
Imprimatur: Reverend Monsignor William Stumpf
Archdiocese of Indianapolis, Indiana
March 2, 2017

Book Layout ©2017 BookDesignTemplates.com
Cover Design by Taylor Slyder
Cover Photo used under license from Shutterstock.com

The Liturgy of Marriage/Timothy Heck

ISBN: 978-0-9979537-0-1
Library of Congress Control Number: 2017938708

This book is printed on acid free paper.

Contents

Disclaimer

The content of this book has been written for the general interest and information of the reader. Names, identifying details, and circumstances of the case examples used herein have been changed to protect the privacy of individuals. Nothing said or implied in this book should be taken, or construed in any way, as a substitute for seeking professional counseling or services of any kind. It is entirely informational, offering readers, educational resources, anecdotes, case studies, and stories. Every effort has been made to offer citations for all direct quotes, and links to appropriate resources and websites. Readers are encouraged to seek out the services of a priest or qualified counseling professional for direct assistance with personal or marital problems and crises.

Dedicated to Margie, my *Karis* now and always!

Foreword
by Ashley Noronha

Rome is the Eternal City; a magical place where busy modernity meets the whispers of the ancients. The mysteries it holds are timeless and its treasures invaluable. So, it is no surprise that people often ask me what it is like to live in such a fascinating place. One can imagine that the city offers a plethora of history, beauty, culture and spirituality. But not many realize that one of the greatest blessings of living in bella Roma is the opportunity to meet so many wonderful people, who traverse land and sea to spend time as pilgrims in the Holy City. One of those wonderful wayfarers is Dr. Timothy Heck. Our nascent friendship blossomed over tea, sipped within the 16th century walls of what was once a Renaissance cloister. And after first ruminating Raphael's "Sibile e angeli," one knew the conversation to follow could only be inspired. As a communications professor and TV and radio journalist, my journalistic sense was intrigued by Tim's deep love of the Church and her liturgy, which he intertwined with his professional pursuits. He shared personal anecdotes of his work in counseling and family practice, clearly viewing it as far more than a career, but as a ministry. He also spoke of his yearning desire to join these loves - the spiritual, clinical and practical. Here, in the pages of this book, Tim seems to have found the perfect union of those skills and passions.

As one strolls the streets of Rome, the keen-eyed observer may notice the recurrence of four ubiquitous letters. The letters "SPQR" are inscribed on everything from man hole covers to coins to garbage cans. The initials represent the Latin phrase Senātus Populusque Rōmānus, which loosely means "The Senate and People of Rome." It is a reminder - from as far back as 80 BC - of the important services provided by the Senate for Rome's citizens. These were the indispensable services such as water, oil, and sanitation, without which the populous would neither flourish nor live. These were called the Senate's "liturgical services." In this book's Introduction, Tim looks at the etymology of the word, "liturgy." When Christianity began to grow in the land, the word was commandeered by the Christians, to refer to those liturgical services provided by the mother Church, without which no Christian could either flourish or live spiritually. The early Christians knew just how important the holy liturgy was. That knowledge is demonstrated time and time again in stories of the saints, when even during times of persecution when the liturgy was banned under the threat of torture and death, Christians took great risks to attend liturgy, claiming that without the holy liturgy, life was not worth living.

It is the same liturgy which points each of us toward the Heavenly Jerusalem, the Eternal City of God; where we hope to one day experience the beatific vision, when the creature is face to face with his Creator. Until that day comes, our benevolent Creator allows a foretaste of that bliss through the liturgy of the holy Mass. When the apostle John experienced his "revelation" on the isle of Patmos, he witnessed how the earthly liturgy was an authentic participation in the perpetual Heavenly Liturgy. Thus, we understand that the liturgy or the Mass, is the most intimate manner in which heaven and earth come together, where Christ is both the priest and sacrificial offering, making it the most powerful, unitive and pleasing prayer to God the Father.

This is why Vatican II refers to the liturgy as *"the summit toward which the activity of the Church is directed and at the same time, the font from which all her power flows. For the aim and object of apostolic works is that all who are made sons of God by faith and baptism should come together to praise God in the midst of His Church, to take part in the sacrifice, and to eat the Lord's supper* (Sacrosanctum concilium 10)." In this citation, the fathers of Vatican II succinctly summarize the importance of the sacraments for the people of God in the life of the Church, without which we would spiritually wither. They go on to highlight the manner in which the Eucharistic sacrifice *"is the fount and apex of the whole Christian life, [in which the priests] offer the Divine Victim to God, and offer themselves along with It.*

Thus both by reason of the offering and through Holy Communion, all take part in this liturgical service, not indeed, all in the same way but each in that way which is proper to himself. Strengthened in Holy Communion by the Body of Christ, they then manifest in a concrete way that unity of the people of God which is suitably signified and wondrously brought about by this most august sacrament (Lumen Gentium 11)." The liturgy is also central to the family: "from the wedlock of Christians there comes the family, in which new citizens of human society are born, who by the grace of the Holy Spirit received in baptism are made children of God, thus perpetuating the people of God through the centuries. The family is, so to speak, the *domestic church*."

The Eucharist, which is the core of the Liturgy, is the 'soul food' that each of us needs to sustain and animate our lives of faith in this earthly battle between spirit and flesh (Gal 5:15-22). "St. Thomas Aquinas uses the term 'repræsentare,' which indicates that the Eucharist is not simply a pious recollection of the dead and risen Lord, who wishes to touch every person, but his effective and efficacious presence. The meaning of the sacrament is threefold: The first concerns the **past**, insofar as it commemorates the passion of the Lord, which was a true sacrifice... Accordingly, the celebration of this Sacrament is called Christ's sacrifice. The second ...concerns the **present** effect, namely the unity of the Church in which people are brought together through this Sacrament...The third concerns the **future**, since this Sacrament is a prefigurement of the

Divine Blessedness to be realized in heaven" (Synod of Bishops XI Ordinary General Assembly, The Eucharist: Source and Summit of the Life and Mission of the Church, par 15).

The nature of marriage too offers this one-flesh unity, which joins the past, present and future. Marriage binds the *past* of two persons who lay down not only their gifts and talents at the altar, but also their shortcomings and woundedness. Through the *present* graces of the sacrament of matrimony, the two are united in Christ who likens the unity to that of Himself, as the Bridegroom of the Church (Eph 5). The *future* they step into will consist of man and wife leading the other into the ultimate fulfillment of their union, culminating in the eschatological wedding feast; the great banquet of the Lord; the marriage supper of the Lamb (Rev 19:6-9).

In this book, Dr. Heck brings the liturgy of the heavens to life in our homes. Through expertise and wisdom from counseling individual adults and couples for dozens of years, he encapsulates the best of research-based treatment models and Christian principles for marriage, while demonstrating the unique gifts inherent to the sacrament of marriage. In his clinical practice, Tim tenderly and compassionately addresses the issues clients face, thus drawing couples closer to a sense of personal peace and satisfaction with life and relationships. In this book, he generously makes those gifts and skills available to a vast audience. The reflections, exercises and questions he provides at the end of each chapter make it an excellent resource for personal reflection, for couples, or for group studies. With a mix of practical, spiritual and theoretical guidance, Tim demonstrates how any couple can make their marriage a fulfillment of the exhortation of St. Paul in Romans 12:1-2: "by the mercies of God, offer your bodies as a living sacrifice, holy and pleasing to God."

This book is also for those who ask, "where do married people fit in the Church?" "How does the liturgy connect to my daily life?" Or, "how can my marriage grow in Christ's love?" This is not a book-in-an-afternoon read, but a gift meant to be savored, as it guides the reader to contemplate the past, present and future, so as to better focus on your Eternal destiny. Whether you are already married or are thinking about it, you will find value from Part One on marriage preparation - which Tim likens to the Introductory Rite of the liturgy - all the way to the book's end, when he shows how to apply his techniques and go forth ("*ite missa est*") - just as the Concluding Rite of the liturgy calls us to do - and to allow the graces of the liturgy to pour themselves into the heart of your marriage.

Ashley Noronha

Ashley Noronha is a journalist, the host of Voice of the Vatican on Shalom World TV, the Rome Correspondent for the Relevant Radio Network and a consultant of Crisis Communications and Media Training for Religious leaders and organizations. She has been featured on TV news networks like FOX, CBN and CBS as an expert on Vatican issues. She teaches Media Training for Priests at the Pontifical North American College and is an Instructor of Media Training at the Pontifical University of the Holy Cross. She was formerly the English Language Official at the Pontifical Council for Social Communications at the Vatican. Ashley graduated in International Business and Marketing from the

University of Dayton, Ohio, holds a Masters in Theology from Holy Apostles Seminary, an STL in Communications and is a PhD candidate in communications and journalism. She speaks Italian, loves a good cappuccino and sharing Rome with everyone from Romaphiles to first time visitors of all ages.

Ashley's husband, John, is the Producer of Voice of the Vatican on Shalom World TV. He is also Professor of Art & Architecture and Theology. He brings a diverse cultural and academic background to the tour experience, with a bachelors degree in Electronics and Telecommunications Engineering, and a Master's in Computer Engineering and Information Systems. John worked for many years in the telecommunications industry leading the Technology and Initiatives Group at Verizon Global Telecommunications, before doing a Master's in Philosophy and Theology. He is a Wilbur Fellow and is also pursuing a PhD in BioMedical Ethics at the Pontifical University of the Regina Apostolorum. Formerly a professional tap dancer, John loves to cut a rug with his wife and to teach ballroom dancing. John enjoys integrating all these different fields and his expertise in Church and Roman History enhances any tour experience!

John and Ashley were married in February of 2008, and have been enjoying living "la dolce vita" in bella Roma ever since. Their passion is to share their knowledge to help others know and appreciate the riches of Rome as much as they do! They have also been featured on EWTN's TV program Vatican Reports. You can learn more about their ministry and contact John and Ashley at their website.

www.johnandashley.org

"Good Christian liturgy is friendship in action, love taking thought, the covenant relationship between God and his people not simply discovered and celebrated like the sudden meeting of friends, exciting and worthwhile though that is, but thought through and relished, planned and prepared—an ultimately better way for the relationship to grow and at the same time a way of demonstrating what the relationship is all about."

—N.T. WRIGHT

Preface

The format of this book may seem a bit odd to you. In fact, from the book's title, you may have expected to find a layout for a wedding ceremony. What I have tried to do is take the sequential elements of our Catholic Mass and use it as a template for exploring how to bring our faith out of the doors of the Church and into the front door of our home. We will use the elements of the Mass liturgy as lenses to consider how to turn our family relationships into ones that are more satisfying, less conflicted, and much more in keeping with the holy design for marriage and family given to us by our Lord.

Drawing upon my diverse background in both pastoral ministry and mental health, I write this book to give those entering marriage and those who are married a better understanding of how faith and the science of interpersonal psychology blend to bring us into the dream of a holy marriage that will please both God and us.

Let me explain how I decided to organize and write this book. The order of the Holy Mass serves as a channel for the expression of our faith in the Liturgy of the Word and the

Liturgy of the Eucharist. Because I have come to experience, know, and love the celebration of our Catholic Mass, I chose to use the liturgical order as a rubric, of sorts, to channel my own thoughts about how to bring that Christian faith home into the context of our marriages. As you go through each section, you should have a strong sense of familiarity with the various sections of this book. And, if you are a practicing Catholic, you will perhaps realize that you are walking through the Mass as we explore the sacrament of marriage.

After each chapter are a series of questions and recommendations for you and your spouse to use in your attempt to create a *liturgy* for *your* marriage. My hope would be that you and your fiancé(e) or spouse would take the time to read through this book together, pausing frequently to discuss what you have read and share the ideas and thoughts it stimulates in each of you about your relationship.

Let me also take a moment to introduce those of you who may not be familiar with the structure and meaning of the Mass to each of the elements and refresh your understanding for you who regularly participate in the celebration of the Mass.

The Mass begins with the Introductory Rites, including an entrance song, the procession of the celebrant(s), the Sign of the Cross, the Act of Penitence, and on Sundays and solemnities, the Gloria, concluding with the Opening Prayer. Then we come to the Liturgy of the Word made up of readings from Scripture. This would include a reading from the Old

Testament, the New Testament (on Sundays and solemnities), a Responsorial Psalm to aid us in our meditation on the word and conclude with the high point of the Liturgy of the Word, the reading of the Gospel. The Liturgy of the Word concludes with the Prayer of the Faithful or the General Intercessions.

The Liturgy of the Eucharist begins with the preparation of the gifts and the altar as the representatives of the people bring forward the bread and wine that will be blessed and become our spiritual food during the consecration. The Eucharistic Prayer includes the words of institution and consecration and concludes with the Final Doxology before the faithful are led to the Eucharistic table to receive now the body and blood of Christ.

Finally, the Mass ends with the Concluding Rites when the celebrant priest blesses the people concluding with the Trinitarian sign of the cross. The word "Mass" comes from the Latin word, *"Missa."* The assembled respond with the words "Thanks be to God!" and the celebration ends with the Recessional.

Acknowledgements

My heart is filled with gratitude for the many people who contributed to the writing of this book. Without all of them this work would have remained just a dream of mine!

To the countless couples who have given me access to the sacred soul of their marriage and permitted me to influence their dance.

To my clinical staff who always inspire me with their knowledge and skill.

To my administrative staff who prepare the path for my clients and support me in countless ways.

To Ashley Norhona for your kind words, editorial comments, and the beautiful ministry you and your wonderful husband, John, give to the Church.

To Marcus Woods for having the courage to speak up to me and speak out in an amazing defense of the One, Holy, Catholic and Apostolic Church.

To Chuck Neff for his inspiring daily show on Relevant Radio, his own powerful book on the life of Father Dan Farley that gave me such motivation to keep writing, and for introducing me to Laura Clark, my publisher.

To Laura Clark for believing in me and taking a risk on this novice writer.

To Most Reverend Timothy Doherty for reviewing the manuscript and his assistance with the *Nihil Obstat* and *Imprimatur*.

To Reverend Monsignor William Stumpf, for his assistance with the *Imprimatur*.

To Taylor Slyder, my incredibly talented niece, for the one of a kind cover design on the book.

To my father and mother for introducing me to the Savior of my life and raising me in the Christian faith.

To my children and their spouses for loving me despite my many failings. You are my pride and joy!

To my grandchildren who make my heart effervesce with joy and remind me why God created us in the first place.

To those whom I have failed. Your pain has shown me how desperately I need God's extravagant grace.

And to my beautiful wife, Margie, for putting up with my procrastination in this work, for loving me when I can be so very unlovable, and for the *gift* that you are to me for which I will be eternally grateful, my *karis*!

"I am nothing special, of this I am sure. I am a common man with common thoughts and I've led a common life. There are no monuments dedicated to me and my name will soon be forgotten, but I've loved another with all my heart and soul, and to me, this has always been enough."

–NICHOLAS SPARKS, *The Notebook*

Expanding Our Understanding of the Faith

TAKING THE MASS HOME

My earliest exposure to the Christian faith came in my childhood home. In those two decades, my father and mother introduced me to the fundamental notion that we are not alone in this universe. There is a God and He desires relationship with us. The exercise of their faith laid the foundation for me to set out on that journey to find this One who seemed so vaguely elusive and distant. Little did I know at the time, it was not I who would find God, but God who would find *me*.

Growing up in a non-denominational evangelical Protestant church, I was taught that we were *not* the only Christians on the planet and that there were countless others who might be a part of that spiritual body called the Church. But I also sensed very strongly that the Roman Catholics were not even close to being a part of that communion. From what I could see and was incorrectly told, they were performing a syncretistic set of legalistic rituals, contrived by human design, corrupted by falsehood, and completely at odds with Holy Scripture.

Four years at a Christian college did nothing to change those childhood perceptions of Catholicism. Two graduate degrees from established and respectable Christian seminaries failed to provide an alternative view that was any closer to the truth about the Catholic Church. And this was my unspoken belief for over forty years.

Although ordained into the Christian Ministry in 1978, I could not feel at ease in a pastoral role. Instead, moved to compassion for the hurting of our world, I gravitated toward a ministry of care and counseling—a much more fitting context for my service in the Kingdom given my personality. Three years earlier, in 1975, at the young age of nineteen, and barely having left home, I entered marriage. Filled with far more confusion than certainty, the two of us began a journey that would eventually shatter and end in divorce fifteen years later. My world fell apart in every dimension. Our two beautiful children were caught in the throes of that disaster and I would come to experience a despairing depression that haunted me for years and still lingers as I look back on my foolish decisions and actions during that season of my life. We all have chapters of our personal stories we wish we could erase from the record but, unable to do so, we then must find a way to incorporate them into our understanding of ourselves and the world to increase in wisdom and reduce the risk of further failure.

Out of my failure and by God's amazing grace, He brought Margie into my life a few years later. She had also experienced the painful suffering of a divorce and her two children were the innocent bystanders in its wake. Falling in love again, this time at 37, I gained a fresh new appreciation for God's gifts of mercy. In fact, to this day Margie and I refer to each other in our cards and notes as *"my karis."* It is a Greek word that can be translated as *gift* or *thanksgiving.* This is what she was and is to me—a precious gift for which I am eternally thankful!

We were happy, contented Evangelicals. In fact, God gave us yet another grace when he opened a door for us to work in a local church ministry. My responsibilities were primarily to preach on the weekends at the worship services, so this allowed me to continue the counseling practice I had come to enjoy so much. Our family made friends at that congregation of faithful Christians who have come to be family to us, many of whom still share in our lives.

Then, one day in the winter of 2000, a courageous young Catholic who knew his faith very well challenged me to take another look at history. Looking back is a journey into a classroom that will teach you more than you ever imagined or dreamed. It shook my world. Most people, including my

Christian family, our friends, my seminary professors, and our church community, did not understand what we were doing when we began to explore the Catholic Church. Eventually, and understandably, the leadership at our church asked me to take some time off and work through my questions of faith. A few months later, they requested my resignation. For the second time in my life, the first being the divorce, my world was coming unraveled. How is it that God could deliver me through the divorce, the despair, the depression and anxiety, even give me a place of undeserved ministry—only to now snatch it away and leave me again in a state of utter confusion?

With countless questions to answer, shelves of books to read, dozens of people to encounter in discussion, I found my head and heart caught in a whirlwind with no end or resolution in sight. One day, while talking over a strong cup of Starbuck's coffee, a frequent practice for my Catholic mentor and me, he responded to one of my questions with a curt insistence that it was time to stop asking questions, stop reading books, and stop with further discussions. His admonition—*"Go to Adoration and pray!"*

Adoration is how the whole thing began. Marcus and I were scheduled to meet to talk about his own life a couple years earlier, but he showed up some 20 minutes late. Apologetic about being late, he said he had been at Eucharistic Adoration. To which I asked the fateful question, *"What's that?"* He gave me a brief explanation and, in my attempt to find a common and respectful dialogue, I told him a story that had recently taken place at the church where I was ministering. In our Protestant tradition we observed weekly communion, the Protestant term for the *Eucharist*, as we understood it. We had a delightful older woman in the congregation who took it upon herself to bake the unleavened bread for each weekly service. What she left out in leaven, she apparently made up for in sugar, because it was delicious. In fact, it was so delicious that, one Sunday after the worship service, I made my way down the hall to my office and noticed a few teenagers in the youth minister's office chowing down on the leftover communion bread. If I'm not mistaken, I think I even saw butter and jam.

I shared this story with Marcus, assuming he would see the respect I had for Holy Communion and express his appreciation for our common ground of faith. I told him outright, *"I was appalled at the irreverence of those teenagers for the elements of the Lord's Supper."* His response, needless to say, took me by terrible surprise. He said matter-of-factly, *"What do you care? You don't believe it's the actual body and blood of Christ anyway!"* And he was right. We were taught it was only a memorial of the sacrifice Jesus had made on our behalf, nothing more.

At our next meeting, he came prepared. He brought me a tape series by a convert named Scott Hahn. The topic—*A Refutation of Sola Scriptura*. Intending to listen to the first five minutes of the first tape, then return it with a lame apology about not getting to listen to quite all of it, I was again caught in surprise. By the third time through the lengthy series, I was taking notes, writing down references, and literally filled with questions. And so it began—a quest over the next two and a half years that taught us how to *swim the Tiber* and make our way to the Roman Catholic Church.

This is not a book about why I became a Catholic, but I will tell you this. One of the most compelling features of our faith for me was the Liturgy of the Mass. That's right—the routine, scripted, familiar, never surprising, always fulfilling Liturgy, which brings us into the very throne-room of Almighty God. To be one with Him, caught up in Him, enveloped by Him, cleansed through Him, made whole by His grace—this is what the Liturgy does and so much more. It is beyond splendid and defies explanation, being the Mystery that it is. And just as importantly, the Liturgy changes us. It is not just a ceremony in which we participate regularly. It is, rather, a transformative experience whereby God divinizes us into the people we were always created to be.

For the past twenty-five years, I have worked in the counseling field as a marriage and family therapist. My specializations are in working with adults experiencing various forms of mood disturbances with depression and anxiety, as well as working with married couples at all stages. Most of them present in some kind of a crisis. In my effort to help them access and utilize all the resources available to them, I delve into their faith. Sadly, even among the most religious of couples, including pastors in Protestant churches, these couples either do not have much of a clue how to weave their Christianity into their marriages or they have failed to do so with any effectiveness that has made a difference in how they move through their journeys of marriage.

Certainly, the celebration of the sacred Mass is an act of our faith, but at the end of every Mass, we are given the admonition to take this grace we have received and live it out in the world around us. When, at the conclusion of the prayer of Mass, we give our thanks to God, it is an expression of gratitude for the opportunity to do just that—to *live faithfully in love*. And, if married, the first priority for that expression is with our spouse.

As I write this chapter, the front page of today's paper leads with an article about the Supreme Court upholding *gay marriage*. It can be political and cultural suicide to even question the idea that a marriage is only a relationship between a man and a woman and there are countless brave leaders who have paid that price as they have spoken out against the challenges to our traditional understanding of marriage.

That understanding comes from God himself, the creator of the institution. A Vatican Council document, in *The Church in the Modern World*, paragraph 48 teaches *"The intimate community of life and love which constitutes the married state has been established by the Creator and endowed by him with its own proper laws... God himself is the author of marriage."[1]*

An unfortunate consequence of the Protestant Reformation, coupled with the age of Enlightenment, was the removal of marriage from under the authority of the Church. Within only a few decades of Luther's proclamation against the Church in Wittenberg, divorce became acceptable under certain circumstances (primarily adultery). Divorce has been the primary way that the Church's control over the sacrament of marriage has been compromised, through the legal allowance of ending the relationship. Secondarily, the right to solemnize the marital union was given to those ordained outside the Catholic Church, as well as civil magistrates. But in recent years, we have witnessed a far more serious threat to the Church's authority over marriage, as the government has now managed to re-define the very meaning of the institution, diluting the sacramental essence of the sacred union of man and wife in marriage.

Authority is central to most of the issues that divide us in religion. I had my annual holiday *guys* lunch with a couple very good friends of mine this week and the conversation eventually turned to religion. They are both well versed and practicing Protestant Evangelicals, one a pastor of an emerging community of Christians that is functioning like a presumed "church," despite his insistence that he despises religion. At one tense point in the stimulating discussion, the pastor made the assertion—"*There is no authority other than divine authority.*" When I inquired about ecclesiastical authority, he rejected any such notion. And yet, he is also wrestling with how to instruct his congregants on proper ethical behavior. My effort to demonstrate the interrelationship between authority and ethics was met with a bewildering resistance.

Authority is a vital concern in any discussion of truth, from the truth about the Church to the truth about marriage. So, to whom has God given the power to govern marriage? It is, and always has been, the Church—the visible presence of God in the world, evident in the ancient cultures of the Jews and still today in the ecclesiastical expression of the bishops in their teaching and pastoral roles. Marriage is the depiction of the relationship between God and his chosen people throughout antiquity. "*The nuptial covenant between God and his people Israel had prepared the way for the new and everlasting covenant in which the Son of God, by becoming incarnate and giving his life, has united to himself in a certain way all mankind saved by him, thus preparing for 'the wedding-feast of the Lamb'*"[2] (CCC 1612).

St. Paul underscores the New Testament relevance of this truth in his writing to the Colossians, where he admonishes that the *mystery* of marriage is like unto the relationship of Christ and his bride, the Church (Ephesians 5:25-32).

The Second Vatican Council drew upon an ancient phrase, *Ecclesia domestica* (Lumen Gentium 11)—that is, the home as a domestic church wherein the life of holiness is to be lived, the children are schooled in the faith, and the love of God is experienced and expressed. This book is written to aid us in carrying out this crucial instruction, to take the grace of the Mass home and allow the Eucharistic grace to change the way we live daily in our most intimate of relationships with spouses and children. And now you understand better why I say that faith is not just for the Mass.

As I said, my motivation to write this book comes from a deep appreciation for the Catholic faith as particularly expressed in the celebration of the Mass, and from my occupation as a marriage and family therapist over the past two and a half decades. Although the couples in my practice have greatly influenced the stories you will hear in the following pages, their names and all identifying information has been modified sufficiently so as to protect their true identities, while retaining the essential realities of their situations that can greatly inform us on the application of these concepts.

Defining Liturgy (*Leitourgia*)

Say the word *liturgy* to a Protestant and he will probably conjure an idea of a boring service of formal religious activity, devoid of any sincerity and feeling. Say that same word to a Catholic and he will probably tell you about the order of the Mass. Like so many of our theological terms, this one is a transliteration of a Latin word, *liturgia*. The Latin is a transliteration of the Greek—*leitourgia*, understood in the first century Hellenistic culture as a service one provided for the sake of the people. For example, if you owned a lot of land between the local market and some of the people living out in the rural community, you might consider building a road through your property so that the people can travel to town with greater ease and in less time. If you did such a kindness for the community, this would be your *leitourgia*.

That helps us with the original meaning of the term, but how does that translate over to the religious understanding of the word? The first century Church borrowed this word to describe the ministry of those who served in the work of the faith. In Acts 13:2 we are told that Barnabas and others *"...were worshiping* (leitourgia) *the Lord and fasting"*. Paul tells the Philippian Christians he will rejoice and share his joy with them, even if he is *"poured out as a libation upon the sacrificial service* (leitourgia)*"* of their faith (2:17).

So what does all this have to do with the Mass? In my earliest years of college, I had a desire to pursue graduate work in the Hebrew Scriptures and ancient Near-Eastern studies. You're probably wondering how I ended up in the field of counseling, but that's another story. My unique background helped me to answer that question and to eventually find my way into the Catholic Church. The key is *covenant*—it's the template through which we can make sense of the entire story of salvation throughout the history of mankind, as recorded for us in the Bible. When two kingdoms were going to form an alliance, or two individuals enter a partnership, or two friends seal their friendship, or a man and a woman enter the institution of marriage—they did so through the establishment of a covenant. In doing so, the two persons establishing that perpetual relationship, as it was considered in antiquity, served as the covenant heads and represented all of those who were part of their respective kingdoms or households.

Sounds very much like a contract, doesn't it? But the covenant is strikingly different. Put simply, a contract is an exchange of promises with terms attached. If you do this for me, then I do this for you—*quid pro quo*. This is also true of a covenant, but even more so. A covenant is not only an exchange of promises, it is an exchange of persons. The parties stand before each other and declare, *"All that I am in exchange for all that you are!"*

There were several components that went into the making of a covenant, including ceremonial rites to distinguish the relationship from all others. For instance, in evidence of the relationship of support, the individuals give a gift to each other symbolic of military support—a sword or a shield perhaps. You may recall this as part of David and Jonathan's friendship in I Samuel. This would have enormous significance years later, after the death of Jonathan, when David found himself sitting in his palace, grieving, and wanting to show kindness to the household of his slain friend. Having found a grandson of Saul out in the wilderness-a young man named Mephibosheth-David brought him to the palace and restored his father's inheritance to him. That youth could thereafter only point to the shield on the wall as the explanation of the king's kindness—a covenant he was part of through the work of his father. This is liturgy!

I could go on in depth about this beautiful practice of antiquity, but will make just one final observation. A man and woman about to enter into the sacrament of marriage do so in the same manner as those ancient covenants. Standing before each other, looking deeply into those eyes of tender love, they pronounce covenantal words called vows, pledging to give all that they are to the other. The promise is not for a day, not for a year, but for a lifetime. Covenant was always considered a perpetual relationship—unbreakable! I read somewhere that the native Americans well acquainted with covenantal practice, did not have a word for what the white man did to them when the terms of the covenant were broken. It was unfathomable that one's word would not be enough to secure one's actions. One of my professors used to say that we don't break covenants...they break us. Anyone who has lived through the agonizing battlefield of a divorce knows the truth of this brokenness. One of the parties will be prone to deny this reality, not wanting to face the truth of the pandemic brokenness in the lives of everyone involved, from the partners to the children to the extended family to the friends to the ecclesial community and even to society itself.

In my work as a therapist prior to the writing of this book my philosophy was simple—people are broken and I want to help God bring them back together. It has its roots in Eden. Think about it—where would you find the definition of health? I go to Eden for the answer to that question. God creates man in His image for companionship—someone to love, not out of need, just love. Man loves Him back and they have sweet communion—oneness. But something is missing. God creates woman for the man. They love each other and have sweet communion—oneness. Until, that is, they challenge the authority of God. There's that word again—authority. Not content to trust in what their Creator gave them, they asserted their wills and discovered the price of distrust.

If health is found in pre-fall Eden, illness is made clear in post-fall exile out of Eden. It is clear in the creation narrative of Genesis that the communion was broken. The oneness is split and their relationships are left with guilt, fear and brokenness. This begins the story of salvation history—God's plan to restore that communion of love. Shelves are filled with scholarly and theological treatises on the condition of fallen mankind. My view is from the chair, seated across from those whose lives are in shambles—whose worlds have been personally shattered by the fall.

It is curious to me that the root word that gives us *integrity*, also gives us *integration*. I take that to mean that, if we are to recover and maintain integrity in our lives, we must accomplish the work of being *put back together again*— integration. From the individual who sits in denial of his own need for a savior, to the couple ensnared in the self-centeredness of a worldly marriage, to the family broken by distress and, sadly, divorce, we are greatly in need of an integrating work. What follows here is my attempt to bring your world back together, restore integrity to your marriage, and rediscover the faint echo of Eden.

Bringing It Home

I shared my conversion to the Catholic Church. Take some time to recall your own conversion or "reversion" to the Catholic faith. Stop and think back to what your own path of faith looked like. Consider the people who played a part in shaping your own love for God and His Church.

EXPANDING OUR UNDERSTANDING OF FAITH

1. Tell each other the story of how you came to faith in Christ. Give your spouse more than just the facts of the story. Tell him or her about what was going on inside your heart, soul and mind. What were your greatest struggles and obstacles in your faith journeys?

2. How has your Christian faith changed over the years? Talk about what may have influenced those changes, whether they be times of increased faith or the struggles in your faith.

3. When you consider your marriage, do you think others look at it as a symbol of God's loving grace and are attracted

to God by what they witness of your relationship? If not, what needs to change?

TRY THIS EXERCISE

Pretend the two of you are back in elementary school and your teacher has asked you to create one of those poster displays depicting your mutual journey of faith. You know the kind I'm talking about where you have one large centerpiece and two sides that open up. On each side let it tell the story of your individual journeys of faith. In the middle section illustrate the story of your marital journey of faith. Use pictures, magazine clippings, drawings and anything else to be as creative as possible with the exercise. And above all—have fun!

ANOTHER EXERCISE

Create a family trait tree for each of you and include on the tree some of the traits you see in your parents and relatives. Discuss how those traits have had an influence on your own life and, at the same time, how some of those traits may have become sources of difficulty or even conflict in your relationship.

PART ONE

The Introductory Rite

CHAPTER ONE

Getting Off to a Good Start

Did you ever wonder how this whole love enterprise actually works? Well, it depends on whether you're talking to Shakespeare, Solomon, or Dr. Marriage Counselor. Shakespeare would have us believe it is a matter of finally discovering the love of your life—love at first sight, right? I recall hearing a father comment about the *appearance* part of a relationship, made one evening when he was noticing his young son's latest girlfriend, a striking woman with a noticeable external beauty. He said, "Well, that will carry you about three months into a marriage, then you better have something else to build on." Good words that stuck with me.

Solomon might leave us with the impression that God's sovereignty is at work in the discussion of how a man and woman meet, fall in love, and end up spending their lives together. Of course, that is wisdom from a man with some three hundred wives and over seven hundred concubines. Granted, the majority of those *relationships* were actually the result of entering into a covenant-alliance with so many surrounding nations at that time in the history of Israel. Still, we have to wonder if our Creator does not play some role in the appointment of one's spouse for a lifetime, given the importance of the marital union.

Finally, Dr. Marriage Counselor, at least one who knows and draws upon the science of attachment, might tell you it is much more of a psychological and physiological process at work. Man sees woman. Woman sees man. There is some element of connection between them. Perhaps it's the body, or the eyes, or the hair, or the skin tone, or any other first-glance observable trait. If we could know the inner workings of the thought processing of both individuals, we would likely read a script wherein some familiarities are being experienced and assumptions are being made. It may be that in seeing her blonde hair, he is reminded at some unconscious level of that pretty blonde from Charlie's Angels—the television show he used to watch as a child—and so comes to the conclusion that this must indeed be an angel who would forever bring him a blissful happiness.

She may notice that he is well groomed and recall that her father always appeared with a neatness and precision that did not escape her attention. The unconscious mind reasons at a level well below her awareness—*If this guy is anything like your dad, you're in store for a lifetime of affirmation and nurturing love. Go for it!*

And our couple is off to the proverbial races. They take the next step, making a bid for connection. He introduces himself to her—*"Hi, I'm Greg. What do you think of their Sumatra coffee?"* She responds to his bid and throws him a bid—*"Just tried it last week and it was delicious. Kept me alert all morning. What's your java of the day?"* You see, successful bidding leads to more bidding. They continue asking questions, making comments and, believe it or not, building positivity in their exchanges. If this pattern continues, we will eventually find the two experiencing an odd and intriguing level of anxiety—separation anxiety. They will feel a tinge or more of pain at the idea of not being with the other person.

They are developing a dedication to each other, and that is a form of commitment that will not only keep them together as a couple, but will keep them in a very satisfied place as individuals. Did you know that couples in love are some of the healthiest people on the planet? It's really true and the studies support it. Unfortunately, the opposite is also true. Unhappy couples are some of the unhealthiest people in the world. Their immune system is much more compromised than that of the general population. That's something to chew on—resolving marital problems and improving your marital relationship will actually translate into physical health. Take a look at some of the research on marital satisfaction and its correlation to medical health and you may be surprised at the strength of the relationship.

The separation anxiety that comes to the partners as they realize it would be quite painful to *not* be together as a couple leads them to enter into the constraints of a relationship. That is, they make commitments that are much more evidential and difficult to overcome to each other. Even the decision to date exclusively is a constraining factor that makes it more difficult to end the relationship. So, imagine what engagement does to the solidification of the relationship? Then comes the wedding and the exchange of religious vows of faith. Now don't get me wrong here. As a former ordained pastor who married my share of couples, I can readily say that I never had a single person or couple step up to the marital altar kicking and fighting about entering the constraint of a legal and sacramental marriage. Here's the way they're thinking about the relationship—*If this person can make me this happy before marriage, can you imagine what marriage will be like? This is utterly incredible and I'm ready to give it my all."*

This is the science of how a relationship begins and grows to the point of the decision to enter the place of a legal marriage. It may sound much too cold and unemotional, but this is some of the science behind the Shakespearian romance.

What do you need to know before getting married?

I have the opportunity on occasion to work with a couple before the marriage. These days, it is normally by the recommendation of a pastor or priest who feels there may be some questions and has some concerns about the marriage. When I meet with these couples, they are like the two-headed monster sitting on the couch in my office. I don't dare even suggest there might be a problem in their relationship, nor do I dare comment on noticeable disparities that could become problems for them, without encountering their defensive responses to how their relationship and future marriage would be different from all others. Even if they are not so bold, they will normally cite numerous reasons why they will be able to withstand the odds. Naturally, I want them to do so and encourage them to identify and draw upon those skills, experiences and resources in handling the difficult matters and seasons of a marriage.

But what is needed for the bride and groom before marriage? I'll let someone else talk about the bride's gown, the groom's tuxedo, the music, the decorations, the reception and all the other fun parts that go into the preparation for a wedding ceremony. My interest is in getting the couple ready for marital life. Much of what you'll find in the following pages are principles, ideas, and resources to help you be better prepared. So, let me just mention a few things that are good to know prior to the decision to enter this lifelong commitment with that person you have come to love.

Maybe the best and simplest way to put it is to say that you should know the *story* of the person you intend to marry. That story starts in his or her home as a child. You'd probably expect that of a therapist—to delve into the background of the person. We do that in counseling because we find that many—not all, but many—of our problems are rooted in those early experiences of life. Those first two decades are the shaping times of our personhood. People in my field have long argued the question of whether personality is a result of nature—that is, genetics—or nurture—that is, environmental factors. If the former, then we would assume that if a man's father is overly compulsive, then it is inevitable that the son will be as well. But if environment is more the explanation for personality traits, then we would want to explore how a woman was raised in her home and how her close relationships played into that personality-shaping process.

At the risk of sounding like a double-minded politician speaking out of both sides of his mouth, I think both genetics and environment play a key role in the developmental process for all of us. As I approach my *older years*, I am intrigued when I observe how I have emulated my father's ways into my habits and patterns, not consciously or intentionally, just intuitively. It just becomes noticeable on occasion and makes me realize I have some of his genes inside me.

I like to hear the family-of-origin stories of my premarital clients. What was it like growing up in your home? Tell me about your father's personality? Your mother's personality? How did they express themselves emotionally? Did they tell you they loved you? How? What was their marriage like? Did they fight? How did they make up? What did you learn about marriage from their example? Sometimes there's a crisis or even trauma in a person's background. She may have lost a parent as a child. Perhaps his parents divorced. Abuse may have been a part of the story. It's all part of the story that you should know before making that fateful decision to marry a person.

Take the time to learn about your partner's values and how they were shaped. Did his family pass along that legacy or did he come to adopt his beliefs and values through certain life experiences? This may be where failure enters the picture. Our deepest and core values may have been forged through the greatest failures of our lives—those times when we violated the ones we had at least professed to be true for us, but now we have come to know them through lived experience. I'm reminded of a passage in the book of Hebrews where we are given a rather confusing verse about our Lord—"*...Son though he was, he learned obedience from what he suffered*" (Hebrews 5:8). It sounds almost blasphemous in one way, as if the author is suggesting that Jesus was ever disobedient. But that's not the point at all. The writer of Hebrews had two words to choose from when he talked about how our Lord *learned obedience*. One term would have denoted the avenue of what we might think of as *book learning*. The other term, the one used here, denotes the learning that takes place through *lived experience*.

Of course, Jesus was obedient, but his education came through the furnace of suffering.

So it is with us: our faith is made strong in the times when we have failed and yet discovered the power of His grace. St. Paul writes along these same lines to the Church in Corinth, admonishing them with the paradox of grace—*"My grace is sufficient for you, for power is made perfect in weakness"* (2 Corinthians 12:9). It doesn't really make sense, does it, particularly in this culture where rugged individualism is rampant? Saint Paul is telling us that the way to perfection, which is another Greek word that just means *completion*, is through entering into our weaknesses and coming to know the all-sufficiency of His never-ending grace.

If your partner has failed in some small or huge ways, don't write him off as a poor candidate for marriage. I'm so glad my wife didn't do that to me; instead, she listened to my story and saw enough indications that I had learned my lessons of faith. We all have a past full of stories. Some of them bring us great pride, while others bow us in shame. Every day I go to my office and listen to those stories and try to find ways to bring healing and hope. Before you enter the marriage sacrament, tell each other your stories.

Do not just look at the mistakes and failings in your partner's life story. Look deeper and listen to discover how she made it right. What were the invaluable lessons that were shaped in those painful experiences? I cannot find the source, but somewhere through my divorce I came across a quote that has never left my memory. It went like this: *Ah, this is suffering indeed. To know that it need not have been. To know that the suffering is a product of one's own doing.* Failing one's spouse causes inestimable pain to that partner, but it may be even more painful to the one who was at fault, as he must live with the realization that he could have made different choices, but didn't. So, if you're contemplating marriage or even just a serious dating relationship, start drawing a cognitive map of your partner's life story. Detail it out and see what you learn of this other person's journey.

Jeff and Christy's Story

Jeff and Christy met in high school as juniors. This was no "puppy love." For them, they were convinced it was the real thing. With only a brief breakup after they graduated and left for different colleges, they quickly reunited and then made a fast track to the altar. Within a year they were pregnant with their first child, the second two years later and, after five years, they were a household of five. The success of Jeff's career in financial planning came at the cost of having time with his wife and children. Beautiful homes and new cars cannot compensate for time together. They just serve as a nice distraction while the real needs of the partners go unmet.

The couple came to see me after one of their most recent fights when Christy told Jeff how depressed she had been for months, even years. He had no idea, not surprising since he worked over sixty hours a week and spent many weekends with his friends golfing and going to the town's professional sports events or watching them on TV. He could more easily describe the features of his laptop than he could those of his wife's beautiful face. She was tired, lonely and depressed, with nothing left for him after being neglected for so long. His first reaction was disbelief, defending his actions as he pointed out all the good things they enjoyed as a family: the house, the cars, the vacations, etc., etc., etc. It wasn't enough for Christy. Not that she wasn't grateful, she just wanted more—an emotional connection with the man she came to love fifteen years earlier.

There are two primary categories of couples who come to marriage counseling. One set will categorize their problems around *communication*. *"We're having trouble communicating..."* Most of them can't detect my sigh of relief when I hear those words. The other couples are the ones where one partner takes the lead and declares, *"I don't love him anymore...and these days, I'm starting to wonder if I ever did."* Those were the words I heard from Jeff's wife on that first occasion of meeting. I do my best to maintain hope as I try to determine the best strategy to garner her motivation to keep trying, or at least to attend another session.

Jeff, on the other hand, was eager to start the process. I never cease to be amazed at how motivated a man can get when he hears his wife tell him the marriage might be over.

He'll jump through hoops, attend marriage workshops, read any book prescribed, pay any price, and do everything possible to recover her love. Unfortunately, though his desires are good for the marriage, his actions are felt by his wife as sheer pressure. Not only does it not work, it pushes her further away. You see, she's been trying to get him to reach out to her like this for years, only to spend most nights caring for the kids on her own, tending to the household responsibilities or being ignored as he was engrossed in the TV or his computer. Now, since her honest and open disclosure of her utter exhaustion with their relationship, she is in control. He will do anything she asks, if he thinks it will turn the tide on this downhill marital slide.

My first order of business with Jeff and Christy was to get them to tell me their story. Curious to hear the facts of how they met, how they fell in love, how they dated, how they decided to spend their lives together, I am even more anxious to watch for any indications of lingering affection— to listen for laughter as they recount some of those early experiences, and to do everything possible to draw out the seeds of that dream that took root in high school. And there it was. As they told me about how they reconciled during college, I saw a faint twinkle in her eye as she glanced at Jeff when he described how he felt being without her during that first year of college. She was visibly touched by his display of emotion, not too common for the financial planner who was much more comfortable talking about numbers than feelings. But, it was a start. For the next three months we worked to build on that seed of hope and they re-discovered what they had lost...and more.

A liturgical marriage?

So, let's get back to this idea of liturgy. Is it presumptuous for me to suggest that we need a *liturgical marriage*? I'm not talking about the rite for celebrating marriage in the Catholic Church. I mean a liturgy for marriage that enables couples to bring the best of their faith into their relationship. As a marriage therapist I draw from a wealth of research findings over the past forty years, particularly the outstanding work of John Gottman at the University of Washington in Seattle and Howard Markman, who has directed the Marriage and Family Center at the University of Denver over that same period. One of the not-too-surprising observations the research has illustrated of couples in satisfying marriages is that they have *rituals* that characterize their relationship. I like to say that a good marriage will have a *rhythm* to it, and hopefully, that rhythm will be in tempo with the Holy Spirit's engagement in our lives and marriages.

These rituals are varied and fairly obvious, if you take the time to notice. The couple has a morning ritual that involves getting up at the same time, making the coffee, toasting the bagels, frying the eggs, blending the smoothie, or whatever represents that couple's desired practice. They don't need a conductor to orchestrate the moves, it happens quite naturally. At noon each day, she calls him to check in on his day. He uses that familiar *name* for her reserved for his use only— *"Beautiful."* The questions are comfortably predictable. *"How was your morning?" "Traffic bad this morning?" "Did you get the kids off okay?" "What would you like to do for dinner tonight?"* Occasionally a new verse or two may be added to the song, but the chorus remains the same.

And so the morning *liturgy* begins. Now, you're probably starting to realize that you have your own routines and rituals in your life. It may be working well for you, establishing and maintaining that vital connection between you and your spouse. But you may also be realizing how lacking in routine your life is. There may be far too much randomness to your days, moving with speed and spontaneity without the necessary predictability that brings a measure of security and even calm, despite the demands. Others of you may recognize another problem in your marriage. You and your spouse have routines, for sure, but they are not in sync. Some asynchronous patterns may be harmonious, in that the partners complement each other, but they lack the conjoint connection of *singing in unison.* But some experience an asynchronous pattern with a sickening dissonance that leaves everyone irritable, weary and very isolated. In this last scenario, the partners are moving through their days, but not with any visible or felt sense of togetherness. The rhythm may be accomplishing the tasks of their lives, but is not bringing them into a liturgical chorus that strengthens the bond of their marriage.

A Mental Health Cold

We often refer to *stress* as the "common cold of mental health." It is a condition that knows no bounds, affecting nearly all of us, too often stealing our time, energy and joy for life. Early researchers on stress defined it as *a response to a demand placed upon us*. The demands may come from our work, (e.g. emails needing responses, meetings, calls, forms, and countless tasks), or our finances, (e.g. bills to pay, accounts to reconcile, retirement to plan, etc.), our families (e.g. repairs around the house, household tasks, parenting, errands, problems, discipline, etc.), and so many other areas of our demanding lives. What may come as more of a surprise is that the demand need not necessarily be negative. Who would deny that a call from the credit card company trying to collect on an unpaid bill would be stressful? But, can you also believe that a raise in your pay would be stressful? Or what about those unavoidable holidays? That's right, they contribute to our weariness and distressed conditions and there's no getting away from them.

Ever wonder what too much stress does to us? Well, the psychological and medical studies are really quite consistent in their findings. If you don't manage the level of your stressors, the likelihood that you will experience a compromise in your immune system, an exacerbation of an existing health condition, or even the onset of a more serious health problem, increases significantly to a point of statistical probability. Translation—pay attention to how much stress you have in your life or you may pay a price with your physical health. Granted, there are certain times and even seasons of our lives where that may not be possible. But, it is the ongoing, chronic exposure to high stress levels that weakens us and exposes us to problems.

Somewhere in the early counseling sessions with a couple, I ask them about where stress comes from in their lives, how they cope with it, and what the effect of that stress has been. A typical response includes multiple stress factors and sources, minimal means or time to deal with it, and at least minor health problems (e.g. headaches, migraines, body aches, colds, fatigue, etc.), as well as an increase in marital conflict. If you're curious how much stress you've had on your life over the past 12-18 months, The Holmes-Rahe Stress Inventory (www.stress.org) is available online if you would like to take it on yourselves. You may be in for a surprise.

God seems to have designed us with a built-in need for rest. A cursory reading of the first three chapters of Genesis reveals that even the Creator chose to take a day off from his work. The seventh day was known as the *Sabbath*, a Hebrew word that could be translated *to stop* or *cease*. What a novel idea— work for a time, then take a break. Though it sounds elementary and makes perfectly logical sense to all of us, it can be the most difficult *routine* to integrate in our lives and marriages. Yes, rest should actually be one of the regular routines of our lives.

I'll let you in on a funny part of my journey into the world of the Mass' liturgy. When my wife and I first entered the Catholic Church, I was somewhat frustrated by those long pauses in the liturgy of the Mass. As evangelical Christians, used to well orchestrated music in worship—including "bumper songs" before and after prayer times, sermons, and any other part of the service—I thought the liturgists were doing a rather poor job of planning. Of course, this reflected a serious misunderstanding and poor appreciation for the role of silent meditation in one's participation in the Mass, not to mention an overly-inflated ego on my part. Not only has God humbled me (a work He is still very much trying to carry out in my life), He has also enabled me to develop a deep love of those silent moments, even wanting to extend them.

It should have been obvious from my studies in the Old Testament poetry literature that times of silence are of great value in our spirituality. A frequent term found in the Psalms is the word *selah*, another Hebrew word that has no consensus for translation among Scripture scholars, but appears to have been a musical insertion placed by the writer, also more of a liturgist, to encourage the reader to pause. In my teaching, I like to sign off on my writings to students with this word—

selah—and I am invariably asked its meaning by some curious student. My own translation—*think about it.*

We all need regular times to stop and think about life. The busy couple who present for their weekly marriage therapy session will often report that this one hour is a kind of retreat from the world, wherein they finally are forced to stop and think about their lives and their relationship. How unfortunate that something so obvious would be so challenging to implement for most of us. If we are to manage the stress our technological, multi-faceted, heavily demanding world places upon us, we will have to find a way to insert daily, weekly, monthly, and periodic *sabbaths* into the schedule.

It will require a deliberate decision to pull this off. The time will not magically show up on our schedules. I dare to say that everyone reading this book has very few *margins* in their lives. Instead, the pages of our days are filled to the brim with activities, most of which are quite good and maybe even honoring of our faith, but just too much and too constant. Our minds, bodies, and marriages are hungry for times of restful recovery.

How curious that I pen these words on a day after our city has been shut down by an overwhelming snowstorm. It is amazing that it takes a foot of snow and sub-zero temperatures to force some of us to stop, rest, play and enter a much-needed *sabbath. Selah*—think about it.

Bringing It Home

We have talked about how vital it is that you develop and maintain routines in your marriage that will strengthen it and give it a rhythm. The truth is, you probably have many in place already. Take some time to talk about your marital rhythm and be open to the evaluation, as well as trying out some new *rituals*.

GETTING OFF TO A GOOD START

1. Identify at least three regular routines you and your partner do on a daily or weekly basis. These do not necessarily need to be spiritual or religious. Consider together whether these habits and routines are good for your relationship, need to be modified or even eliminated altogether.

2. What routines did you participate in with your family when growing up that have *not* been a part of your own family now? Could the incorporation of these activities benefit your marriage? What has kept you from making them a part of your marital rhythm?

3. Take a few moments to think about a ritual you may have observed in other couples, seen on television, or just

imagined. Share it with your spouse and do so in as much detail as possible, explaining why you are drawn to it and find it meaningful.

TRY THIS EXERCISE

Now that you have answered question three above, choose one of the rituals of connection for your relationship you shared and plan to introduce it this week. Spend some time talking about the details. Determine when you will start doing the ritual, how long will you spend each time, how will you remember to do it, etc. Then, in the infamous words of that well-known philosopher Ni-ke, *"Just Do It!"*

ANOTHER EXERCISE

Go online and locate the Holmes-Rahe Stress Inventory. Take a few minutes to honestly go through the items and assess the amount of stress or distress you find yourselves experiencing at this time. Share with each other suggestions for reducing the tension and bringing more restful recovery into your lives.

CHAPTER TWO

The Penitential Rite
Confession is good for the soul!

It has been said the twelve most difficult words to utter for a spouse are—*I was wrong. I am sorry. Please forgive me. I love you!* If only we could all be perfect, we wouldn't need this "rite." Someone once called marriage a refinery for sainthood. Nothing could be truer. It isn't that we enter the relationship with plans to hurt our partner; it just seems to be the natural course of living with someone for whom you have such deep desires, feelings and expectations, at least in a fallen world.

Take the morning rituals of life we were just talking about. How do we get up in the morning? What is the first thing we do? Are we full of energy and ready to go or tired, grumpy and irritable? And who doesn't know about the toothpaste ritual—bottom, middle, random? If we make it through the early part of the day without a fight, then comes the reunion at that evening hour. Worn out from a long day and ready for a favorite beverage and a long bath or excitedly anxious to share it all with your spouse? Like two locomotives headed around their respective bends, preparing for an unavoidable disaster, their expectations take shape in those moments before re-connecting at that often-fateful hour. Some research has identified the hour between 5:00 and 6:00 pm to be the highest risk time for conflict. It's easy to see why when you take all this into consideration.

Now here's a keen paradox in all this—neither spouse *wants* to have the argument. No one's planning and scheming on their commute home how to set up for a good knock down, drag out fight. This only adds to the emotional intensity, as each feels more than justified in casting all blame for the encounter on the other. And here they sit in their big house, kids wondering what's for dinner and the two of them full of frustration and hurt.

Of course, these are just the small breakdowns. But if they happen too often—if the cycle of negativity comes around with regularity, even these small episodes can threaten the couple's happiness. Then come the huge scenes in the arena of a relationship that has grown weak over time from too many demands, too much stress, and too little loving connection. What is even more dangerous for the relationship are the major arguments that escalate seemingly out of control. In the 70s, the National Hurricane Center developed the 1 to 5 categorization rating system to measure and report the intensity of the storm by the type of damage, wind speed, etc. Obviously, any storm that increases to the level that it can be classified as a hurricane is going to cause some damage. But the risks greatly increase with those 3, 4 and 5 category episodes.

So it is with marital conflict. Small arguments are no fun, but the damage is minimal. Hopefully we grow out of the toothpaste variety of quarrels and the towel-folding tensions over time. By the way, someday I would like to conduct a research study among married couples around the preferred methods for folding a bath towel. In my professional experience, I have observed two primary styles, the first being the quick double-fold, common among males. The second, most prevalent with women, is the *trinitarian*-trifold, often touted as a more spiritual method. Regardless of your preferred approach, a storm may be brewing. It may be only a *Category 2 Hurricane*, but too many and too frequent of such *storms* may cause irreparable damage for a couple.

Once the storm has passed, then comes the assessment of the damage. Marital hurricanes are costly—for everyone. Research has demonstrated that some of the most medically compromised people on the planet are those in seriously distressed marriages. It makes sense when you stop and think that our minds, bodies and spirits are all interrelated. Something happens to us in the social world of relationships, it leads to emotional pain, leading to cognitive distortions and negativity, and even contributing to physical conditions involving body aches, headaches, gastrointestinal problems, and a host of other complaints frequently heard by primary care physicians.

Even our spirits are dampened by the destructive nature of marital conflict. The one we vowed to love endlessly and faithfully now has become the object of our anger and the inflictor of enormously deep hurt. This is not what we thought sacramental love would be and yet we feel helpless to turn back the tide on this battle of wants and wills.

This kind of tension is not restricted to a marriage. I was asked recently to step into a serious conflict among staff members at a Catholic parish. The tension would require a power saw to cut, and what is most disheartening is that these are ordained clergy and spiritual leaders engaged in a war of power and resentment. I witness people in struggles and fights almost daily in my practice, but to observe our spiritual leaders caught in the flames of anger is evidence of how the human factor in the equation of the Church can leave the on-looking world disinterested and even disgusted.

This is planet Earth, not heavenly paradise. Remember, we're outside the "Garden of Eden" and weeds have sprung up everywhere. Desires will clash, problems will emerge and people will not always get along. We need not fool ourselves into thinking otherwise. You might find this a little encouraging: marital research demonstrates that occasional conflict is not a concern. The concern surfaces when the conflict is not regularly repaired and becomes too common for the couple. That's why we need the marriage confessional as part of our regular liturgy. So, let's talk about cleaning up after the storm of conflict.

People frequently ask me how I can do the work I do, listening to people in pain, working with couples embroiled in negativity. The answer is simple—*Reconciliation*. That is the dream I hope for and work very hard to accomplish in the lives of all my clients. To see the couple find their way back into the embrace of love, to witness the bickering staff members rekindle a ministerial companionship and a mutual respect, to watch a life blossom when hope is found—these are the dreams I have the honor of participating in through my work. Not always but, when it happens, it is a foretaste of heaven—humbling and inspiring.

Sometimes I have to push the shy, wounded wife to turn toward her husband and look into his eyes or the embarrassed feeling-a-bit-foolish husband to gaze into his wife's eyes. And in that look, my prayer is often answered and they find the love dampened by the storm. It's only the beginning, but it's a good beginning that gives them the potential to build upon.

Conflict in marriage is inevitable. As I said, some research has shown that a certain amount of conflict is, in fact, good for a marriage. The problem does not seem to be the conflict itself as much as the way in which we work through that conflict.

Most of the couples who come to see me have the expectation that they will learn how to better handle conflict. I like to begin with them by clarifying that there are two kinds of conflict. The first is the kind that we can solve. The second is the kind that is perpetual and unsolvable. That's right, not all problems have a solution. Furthermore, not all problems even need a solution.

This is particularly true for women. Let me give you husbands an important tip when it comes to helping your wives handle the conflict of their lives. We've all been there—you ask her about her day and out it comes. She lets loose a torrid of emotion as she relays the happenings of her day with drama and strong emotion. Your response, once she comes up for air, begins the work of solving her problems. This male response makes perfect sense; it's the logical thing to do. Not so much. We have found that as much as 70% of the issues and problems she brings to you do not require a solution, just a dialogue where she talks and you listen...attentively. Take a moment to think about that and let me put it into a formula, because we men do like our formulas. We like to know what the secret is to handling all these problems that will gain us the result we're looking for. Let's put it another way. His wife lets loose with her account of the problems of the day, week, life. It's all out there in front of you like a gallon of spilled milk from one of the kids' many morning accidents. I see it all the time with couples as I counsel them through conflict. In my head, I'm just

THE LITURGY OF MARRIAGE • 69

waiting for his question, that inevitable question every man wants to ask and usually does—*"What do you want me to do?!"* Amplified a bit, it goes like this—*give me the formula to respond to this kind of emotional display that will eliminate the distress for you, resolve the problems you're facing, and bring full peace to us right now so you won't take any of this out on me.*

If he dares to ask the question, using any of a variety of terms and formats, she is likely to look at him in utter bewilderment, which fairly quickly grows to a point of frustration, then makes its way to full-blown anger. She may blow a gasket or she may just shut it all down, stonewall and pull back, making a fast retreat into the refuge of her friends who give her what she most needs—a listening ear. Now they're both frustrated and hurt. After all, he tried to help, but she essentially turned him down, not ready to hear his solutions and really not wanting to make this about him, which is what she heard in his question. Okay husbands, grab a pen or, better yet, get a chisel and stone and start writing—When my wife comes to me with her pain, frustration and hurt, first listen. Assume she does not need you to solve her problem(s). Look at her while she is talking. Pay attention to the story she shares with you so you can make a brief reflection on occasion and perhaps ask a leading question that will draw her out all the more. Then keep listening. Wait for her to come to a conclusion. If she needs you to help her solve the problem, assume she will ask. If she does not, do not, I repeat, do not offer any solutions. If she does ask you a question that sounds like she's wanting you to solve her problem, first turn it back onto her using the infamous *Columbo* routine—"*What do you think, honey?*" Continue listening. Remember, it is much better to fail at problem-solving with your wife, than to fail at listening to your wife!

It may sound a little silly, but try it during your next episode and see if it brings a different result. And wives, let me encourage you to do something similar, but for a different reason. Husbands usually don't want solutions to their problems either, but not because they so much need the gift of active, attentive listening. They're looking for affirmation—to know that you believe he has the means and resources within him to handle whatever he's up against. For you to give him solutions is tantamount to telling him you don't think he's capable of dealing with his stressful enemy. I know that's not at all what you would be intending to convey, but take me at my word on this—that's the message of disrespect he will hear. The male ego is rather fragile and hyper-sensitive to anything remotely construed as criticism. We'll have much more to say about this in a future section.

Imagine, then, that 70% of the problems that come up in your marriage do not require solutions. If that's true, then what *is* needed to better handle these kind of issues that have the potential to gridlock us into near irreconcilable fighting and withdrawal? In a word—dialogue! That's the key. Take the necessary time to talk with each other, sharing what's on your mind and in your heart, then listening as your partner does the same. Better yet, encourage your partner to go first. I'm thinking about some very dear friends as I give that recommendation. Having recently experienced some critical problems in their own marriage, my wife and I provided for them to attend one of the Retrouvaille Weekends to work on their relationship. If you're not familiar with Retrouvaille, please explore their website (www.retrouvailleto.org) to learn more about this wonderful resource for couples to work on their marriage, along with the six-week follow-up group meetings. One of the most helpful take-aways from the weekend was the practice of having a *Daily Dialogue*, where they spend about 30 minutes sharing with each other in a good conversation. If I could give couples just one piece of advice as a marriage counselor, it would be just that—spend at least 30 minutes every day in focused conversation where you listen and talk, then listen some more. It will make a difference, guaranteed.

A lot of people question the necessity of seeing a therapist when life is not going well. Men especially find it difficult to open up with a perfect stranger about their personal issues, feeling embarrassed and thinking to themselves that they should know how to fix the problems and should not need to seek help from anyone else, let alone a professional "problem-solver," as they assume him to be. Nothing could be further from the truth. Therapy is not so much about solving problems as it is about creating a setting where the individual or couple can better find ways to handle their problems on their own. Not too long ago, I read in one of my professional journals an article on the effectiveness of counseling over the previous five decades. We call that a meta-analysis—a kind of research in which the researchers look at the outcomes of various therapeutic approaches and compare their results to see which forms of treatment would be better than others. The findings were somewhat surprising to those of us in the field. Most of us are loyally devoted to our well-developed theories and highly honed techniques. So we read a study like that and are anxious to arrive at their conclusions, which will, no doubt, support our own chosen theoretical approach to treatment. Needless to say, the final analysis was more than a little surprising, though it really shouldn't have been. They found that, while certain models may be more efficacious in the treatment of certain psychological conditions and disorders (excluding organic conditions like schizophrenia, etc.), when you are going through a difficult and painful time of life, it generally helps to open up to a trusted professional.

And there you have it. Four earned degrees, 1000 hours of clinically supervised residency, 26 years of professional practice experience, and it all comes down to that? (Please, for the sake of my livelihood, don't share this with too many people or I may have to learn how to become a barista at my local Starbucks). One of my colleagues puts it this way—*Good counseling is really just a good conversation!* So true, and that is why I spend so much of my time with couples attempting to facilitate them recovering the ability to have that *good conversation* between the two of them. I say *recover* because I work under an assumption that can be easily validated, that they have had these *good conversations* in their relationship history. I may have to take them all the way back to the beginning where they were just getting to know each other, as we described the process in an earlier chapter, but I know it was there. They don't so much need lessons in communication as assistance with unblocking and removing those obstacles that have kept them from having those good conversations over the weeks, months and sometimes years that, ultimately, brought them to me for help. If you find yourselves in a similar situation, no longer able to connect in good conversation, don't give up. Get help from a qualified counselor who will respect the sanctity of your marriage and help you overcome those obstacles to rediscover joy in your relationship.

Having said all that, let's get back to the matter of those unsolvable or don't-need-to-be-solved problems. We like to refer to them as perpetual problems because they will probably follow you throughout the years of your marriage. In fact, stop and take a quick look back over the years of your marriage and see if that isn't true. And I would be so bold as to say that if I met you in another ten or twenty years down the road, you would tell me you're still having those particular perpetual problems in your marriage. The difference, I hope, will be that you learned along the way to not argue and problem solve over them so much, but to have all-important dialogue on a regular basis so you were each able to be heard despite the somewhat chronic issues.

I find it helpful to give my couples a list from which they can identify the type of issues they commonly face in their relationship. Not only does this enable them to objectively label the issue, it also gives them a sigh of relief to realize that if their issue shows up on an actual list of common problems couples face, then they must not be all that bad off and maybe they're more normal than they may have thought. Take a look at the following list and see if you can identify a couple of the perpetual issues that you and your spouse encounter in your relationship.

Differences in Neatness and Organization—One of you likes to have a place for everything and everything in its place, while the other has a high tolerance for clutter and seems to enjoy the predictable hunt that takes place when he tries to find whatever it is he's looking for. As you might tell from the sarcasm leaking through that explanation, we *enjoy* this perpetual problem in our own marriage. No matter how much Prozac I take, I cannot seem to overcome this compulsive need to bring order to the world. I like to defend it theologically by seeing it as an effort to restore a little bit of Eden to the world.

My wife, on the other hand, sees it as a time-wasting effort to procrastinate from focusing on the priorities that matter much more than neatness, like writing this book. You would not believe the countless methods I have at my disposal that have delayed the actual completion of this writing. I hate to admit it, and I'll deny it if you tell her I told you this, but she's right and I'm wrong. Even the theological truth is wrong—we can never get back to Eden and, for that matter, should stop trying. Let's focus on the eternal realities of holiness and heaven, the new Eden, and let go of trying to bring temporary order to our "necks of the world." Don't get me wrong—I'm not advocating messy-ness, irresponsibility, and chaos. I'm saying there's a balance to be sought that will be much healthier in the end and also keep more peace in your marriage.

I should add that my wonderful wife is not messy or disorganized. She just organizes differently—preferring, at times it seems, the *piling system* over the *filing system*, as they say. In my not-so-smart-forgot-that-I'm-a-marriage-counselor moments, I will remind her that she is "over-stuffing" the bags, the drawers, the cars, the closets, etc. Trust me on this—do not try to logically and rationally explain to your partner why he or she should change their lifelong habits and routines. If you try, you might first want to call my office. I think I have an opening in two weeks.

Differences in Emotional Expression—One of you has a distinct flair for letting your feelings be known to others.

You're not afraid to say it like it is, boldly going where no man has gone before, then you feel able to clean up the possible mess later without any leftover hurt feelings. After all, that's how you did it in your family growing up, right? The other has learned and adopted a much more gentle, albeit passive and sometimes, passive-aggressive way of getting those emotions out in the open. Correction, they never really do get out in the open. Instead, they just fester. But, in all fairness, it should be said that in his attempt to hold those emotions within, he is trying to protect the partner from what may be a hurtful display of emotionality.

There are other manifestations of this perpetual difference in partners' personalities. This one is usually, not always, but usually, gender distinctive with the husband likely to have difficulty giving expression to his deep feelings of love, hurt, guilt, fear and other core emotions. Lacking the expression of these underlying feelings, his wife may come to experience an emotional disconnection from him. But, at the same time, those feelings on his part don't just wither away and die. They end up finding other expressions, sometimes ones that are not all that healthy for him or their relationship. For instance, instead of telling her how hurt he is by what she said, he ends up getting angry with her. Instead of expressing his fear that she might be withdrawing from him, he finds himself withdrawing from her. Instead of acknowledging guilt over how he treated her, he becomes overly and protectively defensive with her.

Once again, the dialogue is really the only way to work through these kinds of differences and keep them from boiling over and causing damage to your relationship. Wives, be patient with your emotionally handicapped husband. Give him the patience and time and, perhaps, the coaching he needs to develop a vocabulary for expressing himself emotionally. I will say that this is an acquired skill. We find that women are normally more versed in the language of emotion because of having had such conversations with their mothers growing up, whereas boys experienced their fathers as, well, pretty much like they are now—emotionally handicapped.

One of the excellent resources available in this area for learning and developing the art and skill of emotionally expressing oneself is the outstanding work of author Daniel Goleman, in his work on what is known in our field as emotional intelligence. Head to your nearest Amazon online store and do a search for *emotional intelligence* and you'll find a literal plethora of books on the subject. Research in this field has even demonstrated some fascinating physiological findings on the hemispheric domains within the brain that account for emotional and rational experiences that can be developed over time and with help.

Please note that emotional intelligence is distinctly separate from cognitive intelligence. In fact, there is virtually no connection with the two, though there may be a possible negative correlation with higher levels of cognitive I.Q. and lower levels of E.Q., but this would also be a gross over-generalization that is not really supported in the research literature. Regardless, if you can identify with this discussion and may find yourself a little emotionally-challenged, be encouraged in knowing that you can study up, practice up, and acquire some new skills that will greatly improve, not only your marriage relationship, but probably all relationships in your life.

Differences in Approaching Finances—A common difference among married couples revolves around their way of handling and even valuing money. One of you places a high value on the dollar, while the other puts more value on what the dollar can purchase, resulting in the former partner wanting to conserve and save, with the latter partner more likely to spend and borrow. This is, perhaps, the one perpetual problem that can lead to some serious solvable problems, though not always easily. Once a threshold of spending and debt has been reached, it might require outside assistance and even grave measures to haul the fiscal state of the marriage back in order.

I first saw Brian and Tiffany (fictious names) on the heels of him discovering she had taken out three credit cards in her name and maxed all of them out to the aggregate total of over $30,000. Needless to say, they had some words and many heated exchanges when he came to realize they would have to borrow against their hard-earned retirement savings in order to pay off the debt their creditors were now hounding them to pay. Not only did we have to help them find and honor a plan for handling their finances better, we had the awesome task of restoring his trust in his wife who had been deceptive and dishonest around her actions for years.

But they did the work, managed to pay off all the debt, mostly by nearly exhausting their long-term savings at considerable penalty and loss, and recover a mutual trust in their relationship. You see, Tiffany didn't really trust Brian any more than he now trusted her, but for different reasons. She worked under the mistaken notion that she had to purchase what she wanted behind his back. And, as it was later discovered, most of her excessive spending had nothing to do with personal materialistic wants, but with household and medical bills that she failed to trust her husband to know about for fear it would depress him, given how hard he worked for the average income he brought home as a teacher. Through our work together, they came to see another kind of value—the value of the dialogue to keep them informed and working together on the financial *business* of their marriage and family.

I say *business*, because that's really what is involved in managing a household these days, and it's not easy for any of us. To manage the more minor tasks of setting up accounts, paying bills, handling online user ID's and passwords, all the way to the major tasks of making sure you have a budget and enough income to cover all of today's expenses, plus save for the kids' college funds, the unexpected breakdowns of cars, appliances and household items, not to mention the future savings needed for some kind of income when you are not able to work, requires a strong partnership with a good division of responsibility, along with mutual accountability. Every day that you put off having this important dialogue, the problems mount and it becomes more and more difficult to ever broach the subject. So do it today and push through the fear to a shared involvement on your family finances.

Differences with Respect to Relatives—Now here's a touchy topic for any marriage, the differences the partners have around their relationships with extended family. As they say, you marry into a family when you get married. And, we might add, although you do and should choose your spouse, you do not, unfortunately or not, get to choose your spouse's relatives. Nor do you get to choose the relatives you bring into the marital mix. This perpetual issue can get quite sticky because security and loyalty are involved. Security is founded in the predictability of our lives—knowing we can trust that life will work out and the *sameness* of our pasts provides that kind of predictability. Loyalty is a natural outgrowth of security, defending and even replicating the past to hold onto that security. But here's the catch—the predictable past need not necessarily be healthy or even functional to draw out our loyalty.

Here's a sample of what it can look like. The holidays are a few weeks away and she is planning the Thanksgiving dinner with all the dishes, as well as the setting, the flowers, the tablecloths, the fine china and all the other ingredients of what she considers a perfect holiday experience. What's the problem, you say? Well, his Thanksgiving history is just a little different. His parents were fed up with all the hype around the holidays, so they went 180 degrees in the other direction, going out for Chinese food where they could be assured of running into absolutely no one who would even know what a Pilgrim was. All goes well...until the holiday season comes around and then comes the clash. You can only imagine what that discussion is like, or maybe you've had a similar discussion in your marriage. It might be significant or it could just be as simple as whether you open your Christmas gifts on the eve of the day or the day itself. These issues are as close to the childhood heart as you can get, triggering intense reactions.

Differences in Preferred Activity Level—This one might sound a little odd, but like many of these perpetual issues, it doesn't always present as any kind of real problem *before* the marriage. But fast forward a couple years, more or less, and you witness a couple on the weekends with her wanting to head out on another three-mile hike and him ready to settle onto the couch for a weekend of baseball play-offs.

So, how about it? Did you see anything you recognized from your time together as a couple? If not, pay attention to some of your more common arguments—those fights that keep cycling around—and I suspect you will detect a running theme or two or three. Try to isolate that theme and ask yourself a few questions.

What positive trait was this particular trait associated with that actually helped me fall in love with my spouse? For instance, if my partner's strong sense of organization and order is a constant source of frustration, is it possible you fell in love with his sense of responsibility and integrity? How about the spouse who spends a little too freely? Could that have looked like generosity before marriage?

Given the amount of distress these arguments cause us in our marriages, is it really worth going endlessly through that cycle? This does not say that the issues are unimportant, just that they may not be worth the expensive toll the fight takes on our relationship and on each of us personally.

Now that we have looked briefly at some of the more typical causes of breakdowns in the marriage relationship, let's explore the question of how we reconcile our way through these kinds of problems. That is where confession comes into the picture. We will say things in the heat of one of these arguments that will hurt. We may strike at the vulnerable places in our spouse's life. We pull away in anger or strike out in near rage. These are only a few of the occasions that demand for confession. If not, we risk sacrificing happiness, togetherness and even long periods of satisfaction in our marriages.

Confession is not as hard as you might think, but it does require a humble heart. Humility is a requirement for one to enter into the marriage confessional and make a good confession of healing. Pride—they tell me it is the worst of those seven deadly sins, those mortal sins that can destroy our relationship with God. It is the source from which the other sins take root, grow and find expression in our lives. The worst part of the sin is how it cuts us off from receiving the grace of God, the gift of that covenant of which we spoke earlier, the gift God so desperately wants to pour out on us. Pride can stop the strongest man in his tracks, the boldest woman in her anger, and destroy the most beautiful marriage like an infectious and malignant cancer. The good news is that there is a cure for pride—raw humility. C.S. Lewis said, "True humility is not thinking less of yourself; it is thinking of yourself less"[3].

Time for another lesson, a lesson in how to make a good confession. Another funny thing about my conversion to Catholicism—I love to go to confession, also known as the sacrament of Reconciliation. What a precious gift it is when you consider it. The Almighty God created us out of His sheer love for us, that we might be in relationship with Him for an eternity, only to have us reject Him and choose love of self instead. But He didn't stop there, instead He kept loving us, and out of His love, found a way to show that love and use that love to restore that relationship. That is reconciliation—the sacrament every marriage needs and needs regularly. The Church asks us to participate in the sacrament of Reconciliation at least once a year. My own experience as a

Catholic over the last eleven years is that I need, or should I say want, to enjoy this sacrament of peace at least one time each month.

When it comes to marriage, we may need to celebrate this gift weekly, if not daily. Jesus was asked once by a group of Jewish religious leaders, in their attempt to trip him up and expose him as a fraud, why Moses allowed the ancient Israelites to obtain a divorce. More specifically, the Pharisees tested him with the question, *"Is it lawful to divorce one's wife for any cause?"* He responded by taking them back to Eden and declaring the indissolubility of the Edenic covenant. That led to another testing question on their part, *"Then why did Moses command that the man give the woman a bill of divorce and dismiss [her]?"* And here's the answer of the centuries that takes us to the core. *"He said to them, 'Because of the hardness of your hearts Moses allowed you to divorce your wives, but from the beginning it was not so'"* (Matthew 19:6-8). And there it is again—that deadliest of all the deadly sins...pride!

At the risk of reducing the problem of divorce to an extremely simplistic level, let me still assert that pride, or, as Jesus so aptly calls it, hard-heartedness, is the greatest impediment to reconciliation for couples. Pride reminds us how much we've been hurt; humility reminds us how much hurt we've caused. Pride says we were right; humility says maybe we were wrong. Pride shows no mercy; humility always shows mercy. If I could discover the cure for pride, bottle it, mass produce it, market it, and figure out a way to infuse it into the hearts of couples in distress...I would have untold wealth that could make King Solomon look like a pauper in comparison. Yet, that cure is available to us in the gift of confession. But how?

What do we do before going to confession? Well, what we are supposed to do is conduct an examination of conscience. If you have ever planned, or perhaps been required, to participate in the rite of confession, but not been altogether convinced that you really needed to go, you may have changed your mind and heart once you went through a self-examination. You look into the mirror of your life and come to see your failings, your immoralities, your transgressions and all those thoughts, words and actions that have offended our Lord. And then you are ready to step into the confessional.

So it is with confession in marriage. It must begin with a self-examination. If you're looking for a formal one, the United States Conference of Catholic Bishops has provided a thorough series of questions on their website. Below are a few of the questions you can think about. The complete Examination of Conscience for Married Persons can be found on the website for the USCCB:

(http://www.usccb.org/prayer-and-worship/sacraments-and-sacramentals/penance/sacrament-reconciliation-married-persons-examination-of-conscience.cfm).

Have I cared for my spouse? Have I been affectionate and loving? Have I told my spouse that I love him or her?

Have I been concerned about the spiritual well-being of my spouse?

Have I listened to my spouse? Have I paid attention to his or her concerns, worries, and problems? Have I sought these out?

Have I allowed resentments and bitterness toward my spouse to take root in my mind?

Have I allowed misunderstanding, miscommunication or accidents to cause anger and mistrust? Have I nurtured critical and negative thoughts about my spouse?

Have I manipulated my spouse to get my own way?

Have I spoken sharply or sarcastically to my spouse? Have I spoken in a demeaning or negative way?

Have I been moody and sullen?

Have I bickered with my spouse out of stubbornness and selfishness?

Have I lied or been deceitful to my spouse?

Of course, what pride will do in its attempt to prevent this sacrament from healing our marriage is to shift the focus of the examination from self to the spouse, leading us to examine our partner's conscience, instead of our own. It doesn't work that way. You will always find a way to rationalize your actions if you start by focusing on your spouse's hurtful actions toward you. The path to peace begins with a humble and contrite openness to the Holy Spirit's exploration of our internal world, cooperating with His mission of conviction, leading then to reconciliation with God first, then our spouse.

Case: Nathan and Shannon
A couple who knew how to say I'm sorry

Nathan and Shannon intimidated me at first. It may have been that they were both medical professionals or perhaps the high economic status they had reached over the last 15 years of their marriage. Regardless, they were both tough nuts to crack. They could be ruthless in their arguments—like two pit bulls in a ring, they clearly knew each other's weak spots and pulled no punches in pushing for their respective wills and wishes. Some might say they were assertive, which is normally a good trait to a degree, but I experienced them as overly aggressive. One of the commonly raised issues they brought into the counseling arena was their disagreement over parenting. His style mimicked that of his father, the World War II vet who disciplined with a stern hand and took no prisoners. She, as is so often the case where one partner goes to one extreme and the other compensates, went to the other side of the parenting continuum and compensated for his authoritarian approach with a mild-mannered, high-nurturing, though sometimes permissive style, not unlike her mother and grandmother before her.

One technique I use in the office is what Gottman likes to refer to as the Conflict Play-by-Play, in which we let the two go at it around some pertinent issue while taking notes on their process and then reviewing and discussing it after the fight, so to speak. In fact, he used to have his own counseling office arranged with two chairs facing each other in a corner area that was a step lower than the rest of the room and enclosed by wooden rails, simulating what he called "the ring." After the "dialogue" concluded or he called a time-out, he would bring the couple back onto "the platform" and have the post-fight review. My format is very similar, although there's not enough room in my small place for the actual "ring," the process is the same. It gives the couple the chance to step out of the argument and evaluate what took place, hopefully empowered to take responsibility for how they each contributed to the breakdown.

This technique was new to Nathan and Shannon, as with most of my clients, but they took to it quickly. Many times I will add yet another interesting feature and actually video the couple during the argument, with their permission of course. Then during the review, we actually play back some of the footage as we discuss what happened. It affords me an excellent opportunity to point out hurtful words and statements, as well as looks, and call out some of the underlying emotion that may have been missed during the episode itself. Working with couples as long as I have and having studied the works of some of the leading researchers on detecting emotion through facial expression, it is fairly easy for me to see and hear messages and emotions that are often missed by the partner, especially when that partner is too caught up in his own pressing mission to make a point.

As the conversation became heated, Nathan had become flooded with frustration and blurted out an accusation at his wife with startling anger, *"You're just like your mother! Do you really want our kids to turn out like you?!"* Most of what we categorize as verbal abuse takes place in a highly charged context wherein one or both partners move into a physiological state of arousal, more commonly known as *flight or fight.* Upset, defensive and certainly not thinking straight, we may spew out words that result in undue damage to the soul of our spouse, just as Nathan had done. He bowed his head in the silence that followed and I witnessed Shannon's spontaneous and shocked reaction as she too was speechless with hurt. There was a clear pause in the fight now that left all three of us uncertain what to say next. I spoke first and gave descriptive words to what I saw on her face and sensed in her crushed spirit. You know you have arrived somewhere close to the soul of the person when you see the eyes well up, the shoulders slump and the gaze of understanding. But this time, I wasn't the only one who saw it. I noticed out of the corner of my eye that Nathan had raised his head and was now contemplatively studying his dear wife with tears forming in his own eyes. For him though, these were tears of conviction for having thrown such a painful verbal dagger at his life partner.

It is typical at this point in the therapeutic drama of working with a couple in such pain, that I have to lean forward and nudge them to take the next step, whether that be to have her express the pain she was feeling or to have him to speak the words of repair. And I was just about to do so, when Nathan broke the silence with his sincere and simple confession—*"Shannon, I am so sorry I said that. I hope you know I didn't mean it. Can you ever forgive me?"* I wait for what seems an eternity and pray she will accept his bid to repair what he has damaged in her heart. Even before she spoke the words, her face revealed the relief she felt hearing him take responsibility for his attack. Not only does she accept his confession and offer her grace to him, she takes a huge step back from her position on the parenting issue and starts to agree with him, saying, *"I know you're right...I need to be more firm with the kids and stick to the consequences."* But, now the tenor has shifted drastically and, instead of seizing upon her in this weak moment of her admission of truth on the matter, something he's been trying to convince her of now for the last twenty minutes, he too steps back and says gently, *"I know I'm too hard on the kids. Guess I'm not any better at showing them how much I love them than my Dad was with me."*

It is in moments like these that I remember why I entered this field. They found their way through the battle to the soul of their marriage that was under assault. Not that parenting is a trivial matter, just that no problem, issue or matter should ever permit them to pound away at the foundation of their relationship as he had begun to do, crushing her spirit in the process. I gave them permission to hold each other, as if they needed it, and extend the touch of grace in that heavenly experience of marital love. I knew at that point that they would not need me much longer. They had discovered each other once again and, in so doing, come to value their relationship above all the lesser demands of their lives. I know, I'm a sucker for a good old-fashioned "Hallmark" ending.

Bringing It Home

Repairing our relationships will require humility and courage. From Adam and Eve to the holiest model of marriage you can imagine today, reconciliation will always need to be part of their repertoire of resources. Differences lead to tensions. Tensions lead to conflict. Conflict leads to arguments. Arguments escalate to gridlock, which can result in untold damage for the couple. How we get back into a good place with each other is the work of reconciliation.

THE PENITENTIAL RITE

1. Think about your last argument. How much *damage* was inflicted in the fight? What about collateral damage to each other and even the children? Did you take the time to affect a repair?

2. What are your greatest obstacles to seeking reconciliation with your spouse after a fight? How have you tried to address those obstacles and why haven't they worked, in your opinion?

3. Consider some of the things your spouse says or does in the midst of a disagreement that tends to *push your button*. Now

spend some time thinking about his or her motivation for doing those things and bear in mind that almost no spouse *intends* to cause a fight.

TRY THIS EXERCISE

Every couple has some problems that will not go away. They are perpetual in nature, not solvable. Many of these are rooted in the mutual personalities of the marriage partners. Some examples were given, including differences in neatness and organization, or differences in emotional expression. Brainstorm some of the perpetual issues and problems you have observed in your marriage. Talk about how your response to these kinds of issues has led to hurt and frustration in your marriage. Then devote some time to thinking and talking about how to keep these issues from harming your relationship.

PART TWO

The Liturgy of the Word

CHAPTER THREE

The Gloria
A Relationship that Looks like God

I n 2014 the Catholic Church celebrated the canonization of St. John Paul II, perhaps one of the greatest Papal fathers the Church has ever had in its two millennia of existence. Among the countless accomplishments, he will forever be remembered for having brought to Christianity will be his series of Wednesday audiences over a five-year period, eventually published in one volume, entitled *Theology of the Body*[4]. I must admit to having never fully completed reading the entire work, not being versed in Latin and even struggling with the translation, but I have managed to digest much of the gist of the material through writers like Waldstein, Christopher West and Jason Evert. These authors have each dedicated their careers to the dissemination of this grand treatise, recognizing the value of it for the Christian community.

I mention all of this to draw upon a central element and theme from John Paul II's teaching—that a marriage, like all the sacraments, is to be a relationship that somehow mirrors the very Person of God. Now, stop and take a breath and give some serious contemplation to that *awe-some, awe-inspiring* suggestion. But, more than a suggestion—it is a reality of our faith. It could be said that everything can, in a way, reflect the Creator. I sit here and look out the window at a tree and see how it tells me something about God, His creativity, His love of color, His sense of uniformity and diversity, and so much more. St. Paul admonished his readers frequently, as when he wrote to the Colossians, *"whatever you do, in word or deed, do everything in the name of the Lord Jesus, giving thanks to God the Father through him"* (Colossians 3:17). Our actions will inform those who observe them about the one whose name we bear—that is, Christ. In antiquity, if you pledged allegiance to another, whether a king, teacher, spouse or even friend, you symbolically took on that person's *name*, and your life would be measured by your devotion to that name. A name was more than a way to reference an individual. It was a statement about the character of that person. So, if one acted poorly, it cast a disparaging and negative image of the one who bore that name—on the person himself.

The concept of *sacrament* raises all of this to an entirely new level. Not only do one's words and behavior bear on that relationship, but the very life of the individual is sacramental.

This is what Pope Saint John Paul II is encouraging us to comprehend in his writing—that the very relationship of marriage is sacramental. It tells something about God. It might also be of some help to dissect the etymology of the term *glory*. The meaning of the word is a description of the character, essence and nature of the one being spoken of. So, to *give God glory* is not really to *give* God anything, rather to acknowledge what is true of Him. If I say that He is Holy, I have ascribed to His character a quality of unblemished purity. And that recognition pleases him, because I am coming to know Him better and that knowledge brings me into much greater relationship with Him. He longs to be known by His creation. His love for us compels us to glorify Him.

Let's get back to marriage. A sacrament, in an even more significant way than any other aspect of creation, is a symbol that conveys a reality of God we might otherwise miss and one that is vital in order that our life in Christ be fully expressed in perfection (the Greek term for *perfection* has more of the connotation of completion, rather than our understanding of something unattainable). When marriage is viewed as a sacrament, rather than a contractual partnership between two consenting persons, then we attach a value and meaning to this institution that reveals an essential quality of the Lord otherwise not evident. St. John Paul II tells us that God, in his essence, is a relationship of Persons. The monotheism of the Hebrew people was quite understandable, given their limited base of knowledge through revealed truth about their God. But a monotheistic view of God need not stand in contradiction of his trinitarian reality as Father, Son and Holy Spirit. Not that these concepts cannot seemingly represent a profound dichotomy, one that ultimately led Caiaphas to declare Jesus guilty of blasphemy, that is, asserting His Own Divinity with the Father. Yet this triune inter-relatedness of the three Persons of the Godhead is the truth conveyed in marriage.

Granted, most of us express that truth in a flawed and inconsistent way. We fall into patterns of self-centeredness, pursuing love of self over love of spouse. Yet, it is that other-centered, loving way of living in the marital state that most paints for the watching world a portrait of the love of the Trinity. I am sadly convicted in writing those words of the many times I have failed to demonstrate anything close to that quality of love for my beloved spouse. At the same time, I can find refuge and consolation in believing that His *grace* is sufficient to overcome that failure, to equip me to love as I should, and to restore our marriage to the image it was meant to be. We will talk more of this idea of restoration in a future chapter, but for now, be encouraged that any marriage can be healed through this amazing grace.

Although it has been years now since my father's passing from this life, the grief my heart feels from his death still weighs heavily on me. One of the features of Dad's *glory* was his artistic ability. Forever an artist, whether in his sketching, painting, illustrating, printing, designing and every other function of his life, he seemed to turn everything into a canvas for creation. He passed on some of those skills to me, but even more, he gave me a legacy of *art*. For instance, as a therapist, I find myself often painting a picture in words of the inner life of a client and, hopefully, of the hope that is possible for that person or couple experiencing intense pain and suffering. One of the most powerful lessons Dad taught me was how to correct a mistake. How often it was that I would sit for hours and watch my father do his work, studying his hands creating a thing of beauty before me as I sat in wonder at his artistic ability. Eager to learn and wanting to get closer to the masterpiece, I would frequently bump the table and cause a slip of the pencil, brush or marker. After a brief moment of frustration on his part and a prompt apology on my part, he would speak those familiar words that have served as a constant source of encouragement to me over the years—*"Tim, it's not whether you make a mistake...but how you fix it."* And then he would work a bit of artistic magic on the page, even blending the mistake into the final image. He and I would always know the truth, but the rest of the world would be none the wiser.

The canvas of my own life is covered with mistakes, failures and sins I would whole-heartedly correct, if given the chance to turn back the calendar. Some of them have been life-changers, others just the nagging propensities of a selfish struggler on this path of life in a fallen world. But I find comfort in the words of my father, knowing that I can, in some way, *fix* the mistake and, even more reassuring, knowing that my heavenly Father can blend the mistake into the final image He is making of my life. The older I get, the more I come to relish these words of Scripture—*"I am confident of this, that the one who began a good work in you will continue to complete it until the day of Christ Jesus"* (Philippians 1:6).

The Holy Spirit sometimes disturbs me with His choice of stories to be recorded in the pages of the Bible. One such occasion is the genealogy of Jesus. The gospel of Matthew (Luke is not so blunt) gives a listing of the key and central figures of our Lord's ancestral heritage and includes David, of course—that great king of whom it was said, he was a *man after God's own heart.* But this is not the epitaph the evangelist chooses to include. Instead, Matthew records these words—*"David became the father of Solomon, whose mother had been the wife of Uriah..."* (Matthew 1:6b). Now I ask you, why does he have to identify what most scholars would admit was the worst of David's life? He will be forever memorialized as the shameful adulterer and murderer. Well, consider that perhaps the Holy Spirit through Matthew was trying to give that first century audience and, for that matter, every other century audience, a penetrating message of hope echoed in the words of my Dad—*"It's not whether you make a mistake...but how you fix it."* And even more, our Lord implores us, *If you will let me, I will use my grace to paint beauty into your flawed canvas.* Did he not do this with David? For Matthew continues down the genealogical line until he comes to *"Jacob, the father of Joseph, the husband of Mary. Of her was born Jesus who is called the Messiah."* (v.16). The undeniable truth of David's life is that through his greatest sinful failure came the greatest gift to all humanity—Jesus Christ, our Redeemer! It shouldn't surprise us that Matthew chose this strategy in his writing. After all, he too had a past—a tax collector who, if like most in his profession in that culture, would take his *not-so-fair* share off the top *and* bottom. Like David, he could relish in the grace he had been shown.

May I suggest a profound application of this principle to you in your own marriage? Out of the failures of your marriage relationship, God can still weave a beautiful gift that brings glory to His name and amazement to you as you find again the joy of this great sacrament!

Not all marriages are alike— different aspects of God revealed

Considering this incredible truth of how our marriages reflect the Glory of God, we must resist the urge to create a *cookie-cutter* approach to the sacrament. One day, by His divinely given grace, we will see Him in all of His beatific Glory, but until that day, we see Him in bits and parts and pieces. We look around at nature, as I'm doing right this moment—glancing at the foothills of the Pikes Peak region of the Rocky Mountains, and we see something of God. Every morning, as the Psalmist sings out, His mercies are new. The face of a newborn infant brings us to wonder at the Creator's design. And so it is with marriage. Each expression of the marital sacrament illustrates the nature of our Lord in its own distinctive manner.

I have read some books on marriage wherein the author(s) lay out a blueprint for the relationship that reminds me of how a dance instructor once tried to teach me the art of dancing—by laying out pieces of plastic on the floor resembling feet, then instructing me to step here, then here, then here. The fact is, I never really did learn how to dance. But, I do know the steps— big difference! Two words still ring in my ears from that ill-chosen experience: *"Loosen up!"* Well, in reading some of the *Do-it-this-way-and-your-marriage-will-be-fine* books, I want to shout out that same encouragement—*Loosen up!* Let the couple dance and work out their own dance as they prefer. Don't misunderstand me here. There are some clearly laid-out principles for marriage and certainly some godly guidelines to be observed, but that is a far cry from giving couples a rigid prescription of how to dance together in their relationship.

I like to think of the couple's relationship as a personality of its own, fashioned and being fashioned by the two individuals themselves, who are hopefully each dancing in tempo with the Holy Spirit. Their dance takes on a personality that is distinctly theirs, with a rhythm that might remind us of other marriages, but is uniquely their own design. And in that design, we observe, experience and engage to the point that we see God in their dance. During my first session with a couple I give some of the basics of how counseling works. Marriage counseling is a little different from individual therapy, in that neither the husband nor the wife are my patients. Rather, I serve the best interest of the marriage itself. That's right—the marriage relationship is the patient. Too often she is dying at the expense of the partners' individual interests. Years ago, very early in my work, I was counseling a young couple who were going at it hard and beating up on each other in ways that drew out my own frustration and defensiveness for their marriage. At one point, one of them came up for a breath from their bickering, looked at me, and asked me abruptly—*"What's wrong with us?"* Without thinking, which is when I not infrequently do my best work, I blurted back in a not-so-therapeutic-neutral fashion—*"You're both selfish!"*

That was well over twenty years ago and I was forest-tree/green-behind-the-ears, but it may have been one of those inspired moments when I let the Wonderful Counselor use me to speak a word of truth into this young marriage. Selfishness is a destroyer of marriages, forcing the relationship to succumb to the self-centered desires of one or both partners, without due consideration of the other. It probably sounds trite to say it, but marriage is to be a mutual give-and-take relationship. C.G. Jung was fond of characterizing the healthy state of the individual as one of *balance*. This reminds me of what one of my graduate school professors used to say—that extremism may be the worst form of sin. Moving too far from one side to the other not only disturbs the balance of the relationship, it causes polarity and even chaos. Show me a marriage where one partner is the primary giver and the other the primary taker, and I will show you a relationship that is full of cracks, flaws, resentment, distress and is very much at risk, and if it is not now, it will be at some future time, unless balance is restored.

A "God-Consciousness" in Marriage

Somewhere along the way I find myself talking with couples about having a "marriage consciousness." What I mean to convey to them is the continual need for them to keep the partner and the relationship in their ongoing awareness. Research has demonstrated that couples in highly satisfied marriages will use the first-person plural "we" much more often in their language, than the first person singular "me." For you non-English majors, let me illustrate in the dialogue statements found in the table on the next page:

LOW SATISFACTION COUPLE	HIGH SATISFACTION COUPLE
"Give me a call when you get a chance. I'd love to get together."	*"Give us a call when you get a chance. We'd love to get together."*
"I'm heading to Chicago this weekend."	*"We're heading to Chicago this weekend."*
"Thanks for bringing my little grandson to see me."	*"Thanks for bringing our little grandson to see us."*

You may be thinking this is scripted and formulaic and you might be right. Nevertheless, it is one of those peculiar findings that emerges from the study of couples. It reflects the marital personality and the marriage consciousness. Without it, the partners are tempted to presume upon the other—essentially, taking the other one for granted. You men may hear this and immediately translate it into the idea of being "hen-pecked" by your wives, yet it is really a manifestation of being in sacramental relationship to and with your spouse. Here's a simple idea to try out. Try catching yourself over the next two weeks and make a conscious effort to use the first-person plural in your conversation—we, our, us... It is a great way to develop that marriage consciousness.

Bringing It Home

Have you accepted the teaching of the Church as given us by St. John Paul II on the sacredness of marriage? I think all of us would have to admit our relationships are a bit estranged from the image of God depicted in *Theology of the Body* and yet that should not preclude us from imagining what it would be like to have a marriage, which mirrors the Person of our Creator.

THE GLORIA

1. What is the first thing God would point out to you that needs to change about your relationship to make it more God-like?
2. If you made such a change in your relationship how would that affect other areas of your life? Your children? Your work? Your ministry in the parish and community? Your friendships?
3. If God's grace shines through our flaws and weaknesses, as well as our strengths and gifts, what will be the greatest display of His grace in your life and in your marriage? To

put it another way, what failures of your lives will give God the opportunity to shine through with His astoundingly amazing grace?

TRY THIS EXERCISE

Draw a horizontal line across a sheet of paper. Label it *"Our Marriage."* Put the date you met on the left side of the line and today's date on the right side of the line. Now stop and ask God to show you the times in your marital history where you failed the most and where His grace was most evident. Make this a meaningful experience of joining together in celebrating God's mercy at work in your mistakes.

CHAPTER FOUR

The Old Testament
Dusty Manuscripts with Convicting Truths

A professor in my early seminary studies was an incredible scholar, teacher and mentor. My poor efforts at understanding the faith are no measure against his highly-respected contributions to the field of Scripture study. With his five earned degrees, at least two from Ivy League institutions, it came as no surprise that he was asked to participate on the team of translators for one of the more popular versions of the Bible in the Protestant world—the New International Version (NIV). In one of his lectures he shared with us that he planned his life out in three stages. The first would be the stage of preparation in which he would complete his education, which he did. The second would be the stage of teaching, which he did. And the third stage would be his involvement in mission work around the globe, which he did.

Few of us accomplish what Dr. Foster did in planning and executing his life plan. I suspect that a private conversation with him might reveal the truth that his plan probably hit upon some snags along the way. Nevertheless, he stayed the course and carried out his work.

I, on the other hand, graduated from high school with little idea of what I wanted to be when I grew up. My parents insisted I must attend a Christian college for at least one year, following in the footsteps of my older brother, which I did. The exposure to instructors like Dr. Foster compelled me to not only complete my undergraduate work in Christian Ministries, but to plan to enter the ministry as one of those instructors. Another professor of mine, Dr. Hooks, who taught Old Testament and Hebrew, inspired me to pursue graduate work in the field of Old Testament and Hebrew Studies. So, I set out on that course, completing my first master's degree in Old Testament and Hebrew, intending to complete a terminal degree at Hebrew Union College in Ancient Near-Eastern Studies, so I could find a teaching post in a graduate seminary.

And it just might have worked, were it not for people. Let me explain. To help pay the bills, I took a position as an associate minister at a local church in Cincinnati. Pastors, priests, rabbis and all other religious leaders have always been the first line of defense against personal, marital and family problems. Studies demonstrate that more than 60% of those who first seek out some type of professional help for such issues first turn to their religious community. It doesn't really matter whether the leader is qualified, experienced, or even willing to serve in such a capacity, for he will still be viewed as a source of wisdom and healing. Yours truly was about as unqualified as they come, but that didn't seem to deter folks from seeking me out for help. Unfortunately, not a single one who came to me in those early days had a desire to learn more about the ancient near-eastern covenantal practices, declining Hebrew verbs, or discuss the factors leading to the divided kingdom. That realization was the key impetus for me to change my career course. Unlike Dr. Foster, I made a serious detour that took me into the field of psychology, preparing me to work as a psychotherapist for the past twenty-five years.

One of the motivations to change direction with my ministry was the realization that I was becoming somewhat *irrelevant*. Although an introverted personality, the *ivory towers* of the scholastic world were taking me out of the realm of working closely with people. Through those early days in ministry I discovered a strong compassion and compulsion to bring encouragement and support to those who are hurting and in need. That motivation continues to drive me to do what I do and it is enormously rewarding, though disheartening at times when my limits exceed the need.

What is uncanny is how frequently I have been able to draw upon that background in the Old Testament. Now let's be honest—most people find the Old Testament to be more than a little boring, distasteful and altogether confusing. That is all true, to an extent, but it is also a storehouse of truth, life narrative, wisdom, and even beauty.

Marriage *before* and *after* Eden

Let's take another brief look again at the Eden narrative and the first marriage. One would think that two adults created in perfection, living in paradise and saturated in the presence of the Creator would be able to succeed at marital bliss. Not so. We are not told how long a period passed between the creation and the *Fall*, as it has been theologically termed. All we know is that there came a point at which temptation entered the garden. The Tree of Knowledge was a place of distrust—a point of discontentment and intolerance with the sovereignty of God and a bite into self-centered autonomy. The tempter ensnared them with the deception that the Creator is not as good as they thought Him to be and therefore, cannot be trusted to do what is in their best interests. The only answer—take matters into your own hands and govern your life by your own ideas of what will be good for you.

The text tells us the woman "*saw that the fruit of the tree was good for food and pleasing to the eye.*" The term "seeing" in the Hebrew often denotes a spiritual experience in which one can envision realities otherwise hidden. The prophet is called the *seer* throughout the Old Testament because he can see into the mind of God. He would then take what he saw and relay it to the people in a manner that led most of them to realize he was the *mouthpiece* of God. Consider that what we see affects our view of the world, shaping our mental attitude about life. In that moment, the woman entered an altered worldview in which her beloved Lord was now seen to be a selfish tyrant withholding goodness from her. The sadness of the account is only surpassed by its continual repetition throughout history.

But there is another striking part of the story that reveals the beginnings of a marital breakdown—the silence of her husband. We see from the reading that Adam was part of the scene. When the words *"...her husband, who was with her..."* are used, the grammatical structure indicates a proximity to Eve that places him in her presence for the entire act. Yet, despite what he knew of God, despite his experience in His grace, and despite his knowledge of the truth that was being challenged, Adam said nothing. Perhaps he had a fear of snakes or maybe was shocked by the whole encounter, nevertheless, he abandoned his wife to the snare of the evil one who targeted her with a cunning temptation. I realize this might conjure up those old sitcoms where the wife and husband are upstairs in bed and she hears a thump downstairs. Quickly, she wakes up her sleeping husband and pushes him out the door to go down and find out what all the commotion is about. He, being a dutiful husband, dons the first thing in sight to cover himself, his wife's bathrobe and slippers, and reticently makes his way down the stairs, but not before grabbing his Louisville Slugger he always keeps hidden under the bed. And so it goes.

All that sounds a little chauvinistic perhaps, but it does have a basis in Scripture. From the outset of creation, the man was to stand in a place of protection for his wife, defending her against the allure of the adversary and pointing her always back to the loving Creator. Adam failed to do so and we have all paid the price ever since. Now, in all fairness to him, I will add that some Scripture scholars will point out that the term translated "serpent" can also be translated as "reptile" or even "dragon." That does up the ante a bit on the scare factor, but it would also greatly magnify the intensity of the threat to his dear wife...a threat he chose to shy away from, leaving her utterly exposed to be preyed upon by Satan.

These opening pages of the Word of God demonstrate so aptly for us how relevant the Old Testament can be for us, even in the context of our marriages. Let me assure you that you can find in the pages of the first forty-six books of the Bible all the melodrama, psychodrama, and any other kind of drama you could ever imagine. Hollywood has nothing on the stories we encounter in this book. And that is why we must do more than just doze off during the readings at Mass. Of course, some of the passages are easier to follow than others and some lectors do a better job with the reading than others. But, let me encourage you to develop a practice of reading through all of the readings some time during the week before the Sunday Mass. Not only will your mind then be familiar with the reading when you hear it during the Mass, you may discover a deeper and more personal application of the passage from having spent that time in the text before the Liturgy.

It is so easy these days to do so, since we have them readily available on our computers, laptops, tablets, and phones through some excellent apps that take all the confusion out of reading the Missal. I will, however, have to admit that there is something rather meaningful in using the actual book-with-paper version of the readings in your Bible or missal. But, please do whatever will work for you and your spouse. And let me also say that it would probably be best that you not just say you'll do the readings "some time during the week," but assign and keep a particular day and even time for the practice, so it has a much better chance of becoming a regular part of your marital routine. Along with that, I recommend locating a place in your house where you can create a sort of sanctuary for the two of you to meet together and with the Lord. It certainly doesn't need to be a shrine with candles and icons, though a crucifix and a statue of the Blessed Mother would be nice, but it should be a place with a couple soft chairs where the two of you can sit comfortably for 30 to 60 minutes and share time together in some of these recommended exercises.

Just a few more comments about the *Edenic* story. The text tells us "*the woman saw that the tree was good to eat and pleasing to the eye*" (verse 6). At the risk of sounding offensively simplistic, let me note that she made a terribly poor assessment of what is good. We all do it and we do it regularly. I can't help but think of my 18-year-old son as I write this. Here's a familiar dialogue with him as we meet up in the afternoon.

Me—"*How was your day?*"

Son—"*Good.*"

Me—"*Really? What was good about it?*"

Son—"*Not much.*"

Me—"*What'd you have for lunch?*"

Son—"*A burger.*"

Me—"*How was it?*"

Son—"*Good.*"

The word "good" shows up some seventy-eight times on any given day in the course of a dialogue with that young man. Here's my point—we need to be much more discretionary about what we determine to be *good* in our lives. We all are guilty of allowing too many temptations to creep into our worlds. They come at us from the media, the internet, Madison Avenue sales attempts, the stock market, and even our well-intentioned friends. But we have a moral obligation to maintain high standard filters on what we permit to enter our homes, our minds and, most certainly, our spirits. Trusting in God means that we do not have or assume the prerogative to determine what is good, rather we ought to trust in His declarations of goodness.

In that vein, I come across not a few Catholics who are quite bold in asserting their dissatisfaction and even disagreement with some of the teachings and disciplines of the Church that have an application on their lives. Just yesterday I was talking with a fallen-away Catholic and she asked me, *"Has the Catholic Church adjusted its teaching about married couples using contraception?"* Her question reflected the mistaken ideas so many people entertain about, what they assume to be, the transitory nature of the teachings of the Church. Although I did talk to her about Natural Family Planning (NFP), I wanted to make it clear that NFP is still not to be used by couples as a way of closing themselves off to life, which is such a central part of marital consent. The label used at times for these naïve folk is "Menu Catholics" because they prefer to approach the faith as if they were moving along the theological cafeteria line, making selections based on their spiritual appetites, rather than trusting in God, through Mother Church, to plan out our spiritual diet according to a Divine understanding of our truest needs. Like the first time we took a bite of spinach (particularly the boiled variety that tastes more like seaweed than real food), we may want to spew it out because of the poor taste, but Mother knows it is good for us and instructs us to eat it anyway. Like fine wine that may taste a little bitter at first, we must develop and acquire an appetite for the gifts the Church provides us in her moral teachings, especially in the arena of marriage and family.

The tragic melodrama of David and Bathsheba

Before we leave this discussion of the Old Testament, let's talk about some very practical teachings and stories from its pages. What comes to your mind when you hear the name *David* from the Bible? If you're like many people, you associate this ancient King of Israel with a woman named *Bathsheba*. Such a sad legacy, don't you think? We earlier referred to the adulterous relationship the two of them had and how God, in His providential grace, was still able to use this terrible and sinful tragedy for good in the story of our salvation. Let's explore the account to better comprehend how adultery can make its way into the sanctity of marriage and nearly destroy the essential beauty given in the sacrament.

In the second book of Samuel the Prophet, we are given the record of the couple's journey into infidelity, deceit and even murder, in their case. It began with King David, who had replaced Saul as the king over all the nation of Israel, which was vast and growing rapidly, some 1100 years before Jesus was born. Most of that growth was the result of the valiant warfare of David, which began when he bravely volunteered to take on the giant named Goliath, despite David being only a youth at the time. You probably know the story of how the boy shamed, not only all the militia of Israel, but also the king at the time, a man named Saul, by responding to the giant's taunts during a kind of "pre-game" battle ceremony against the Philistines. It was really a form of psychological manipulation to rob the losing army of their confidence to win the battle after they've witnessed one of their soldiers lose a personal battle against one of the enemy. But David was not going to let that happen and so ran head-first against any fear, armed only in faith and having the meager weapon of a sling and five stones. And, as the story goes, not only did the lad win the pre-game show and slice off the head of the arrogant giant with the enemy's own sword, the Israelites prevailed over their long-time enemies, the Philistines.

By now you're probably curious what all this barbarism has to do with marriage and that would be a good question, not to mention a nice way to get me back on target given my tendency to wander off into these Old Testament stories I love so much. What I want you to first understand in the Bathsheba story is that David was first and foremost a leader of men in combat. In fact, that is why the Lord denied him his dream of wanting to build a Temple for God. As an aside, note that our Heavenly Father does not always honor our personal dream; rather he shapes it into his own sovereign dream. Back to the story—the slide into gross immorality on the part of David began when he made a fateful decision to *stay home from work*. You heard me right. Here's the way the Bible records it: "*At the turn of the year, the time when kings go to war, David sent out Joab along with his officers and all Israel, and they laid waste the Ammonites and besieged Rabbah. David himself remained in Jerusalem.*" (2 Samuel 11:1).

The king was not where he was supposed to be and not doing what he was supposed to be doing, basically shirking his responsibilities in favor of whatever personal interests he may have had at the time. I would like to give him the benefit of the doubt and assume this was not a deliberate plan on his part, devised much earlier and with intent to commit adultery. This is consistent with my work with couples where one has engaged in an extra-marital relationship. It was not his or her intent to enter the relationship illicitly and begin an affair, instead it found its inception with some foolish, imprudent choices, including one like King David—being in the wrong place at the wrong time.

In modern times, it may take the form of surfing the internet when we should be working on a project, or flipping on the television when we should be studying, or stopping off at some "questionable club" for lunch with the guys when we should be eating the sandwich your wife made earlier that morning. Before we were fortunate enough to have some new carpet laid in our offices, I had a rug in the center of my room to cover up some of my spilled coffee stains on the floor. That is one of my own vices—coffee. Nothing like a good, steaming hot, and strong cup of java. Not infrequently I would have couples in front of me for counseling, attempting to find their way back from an extra-marital relationship on the part of one spouse. Usually several sessions will be devoted to the issue of how this happened in the first place. You see, I don't think in my twenty-five years of counseling couples, I have ever had an evil person as a client. Not evil, just foolish, like we all can be at various times in our lives, present company included. So, in trying to dissect the person's fall into infidelity, I would point to the rectangular piece of carpet rug on the floor and say to them, *"Suppose this rug represents marital fidelity. You can take multiple steps in any direction and not actually step off the rug. But, after you have taken too many steps toward the edge, it just takes one more step to cross the line."* Then we begin to explore those foolish steps and help them develop better boundaries to protect their marriage, as well as their individual integrity.

I recall one case where the couple came in for their first session, the sad catalyst having been a night of sexual impulsivity on the husband's part with his secretary while his wife was out of town, visiting family. Separate travel can pose a threat to marriage partners. Many men and women who have to travel frequently for their work will report how an adulterous night or relationship began with a drink after dinner with one of the female co-workers while out of town. Of course, you say the person in that case was at the right place, wasn't he—working? Well, perhaps he was, but it was after-hours and alcohol was part of the equation, rarely an ingredient to shore up integrity under such circumstances. One of the very practical precautions we can make in those situations is to use technology for the benefit of our marriages. For instance, have one or two daily FaceTime chats with your spouse while away. Exchange texts throughout the day, especially when in one of those potential places of temptation. It's amazing how difficult it can be to do anything remotely hurtful to your life partner when you are texting, talking, emailing, or FaceTime-ing with her.

Let's get back to my client who had the "one-night-stand" with his administrative assistant. I asked him to tell me about the culture of his place of business, of which he was the sole owner. Several of his comments stood out to me in his description of the environment of their office. First, they had a practice of getting together after hours as a group, or at least some of them, on one or two nights a week. Because it was immediately after closing time, spouses were not typically part of the informal gathering. There's nothing immoral about omitting spouses, but it does shift from a working relationship to a casual, social relationship. Again, nothing immoral about that, but it creates what we call in professional mental health arenas a "dual relationship", wherein you now have two kinds of relationship with the person. In his case, he now is relating to his co-worker as both an employee and a social friend and it can be more challenging to keep the roles straight. If it sounds like I'm advocating unfriendliness in the workplace, nothing could be further from the truth. That should be part of our relational demeanor at all times. We're referring more to the after work and alternative context kind of setting.

Another part of the work culture that emerged from the discussion, and I think it was his wife that brought this up, having overheard things said on occasion, was they had allowed people to share off-colored comments, jokes, emails, and Facebook postings, some of which were more than a little sexually suggestive. No harm done, you might say, but maybe more harm that we at first think. Doing so opens the door to impropriety and even impurity, not to mention that anything of a sexual nature will convey a clear de-humanizing and objectifying of anyone being sexualized in a joke, story, picture, etc. It starts to profane sexuality from the holy act of love it is to be within the marital bed.

One other note about this man's work culture that came up during one of the sessions was that this secretary had gone through a divorce that left her in a difficult and strained financial position. She was accustomed to approaching my client, her employer, to request an advance on her salary. She also shared her painful experiences and struggles out of the divorce as somewhat of her rationale for the request. His consent to provide that gesture of support to her opened the door then to her asking for loans from him, which he also gave to her, some of which were known and agreed upon reluctantly by his wife. Others were not disclosed to her, out of his fear that his wife would not approve. This dynamic blurred the boundaries and created multiple, not just dual, relationships with the woman. At this point, he is her employer, her co-worker, her casual friend, her informal counselor, and her creditor-banker. All in a climate that had become less than formal, open to inappropriate dialogue and joking, not to mention that he would have her drop off business papers and items on occasion to his house. This last practice was the one that set the stage for his one-night stand of infidelity with the woman while his wife was out of town. He made the fateful decision to invite the woman into his home when his wife was away, have a drink, talk, and one thing led to another and to another and, ultimately, to his fall from morality, clearly stepping off the proverbial rug.

Returning to the David and Bathsheba saga, one thing is very clear to us, or it seems it should be—people have not changed all that much since the beginning of time. Sexual impropriety is arguably the greatest and most effective tool in the satanic arsenal to break, destroy and steal the joyful integrity from the sacrament of marriage, as well as the individual. And, if I may add another ancillary comment, it has also been evil's way of destroying the integrity of a man's priesthood as we have seen with the scandals over the past two decades in the Church. What better way to destroy both vocations than to attack something so central to the identity of the person.

THE LITURGY OF MARRIAGE • 127

That is not to say Bathsheba was innocent on her part. Despite the ancient customs, she seems to have been flaunting her beauty in the face of her king and all the while her husband was away doing the work David was shirking. Such a sinful paradox—that the front-line warrior in the army had far more integrity to do the right thing than the king himself, yet he was being maligned, betrayed, abandoned and eventually killed for his integrity. As you might notice, Uriah was a Christ-like figure, what we refer to as a *type* of Jesus, who was also maligned, betrayed, abandoned and eventually killed for His integrity, and all for our sake—the ones who deserved what he received. I would encourage you to read the full account of the tragic story of David and Bathsheba (2 Samuel 11 – 1 Kings 1). You will see countless lessons to be learned for all of us, which is precisely what the Old Testament affords Christians today. St. Paul reinforces this truth in his letter to the Romans—*"For whatever was previously was written for our instruction, that by endurance and by the encouragement of the scriptures we might have hope"* (Romans 15:4).

The term used in the Scriptures for *encouragement* renders a much deeper meaning than we might consider. We think of encouraging someone as helping them to feel good, right? But that's not consistent with how it is used by the Holy Spirit in the Word. Encouragement is always to be recognized as relating to another person in a manner that leads them closer to God himself. That brings an entirely new perspective on the action of encouragement. Take, for example, the case I spoke of earlier with the business leader caught in the throes of a tempting relationship. What if you were a friend, co-worker or even a spouse to that man? How would you *encourage* him? St. Paul, in another New Testament letter, gives us a fairly strong admonition in such cases—*"Brothers, even if a person is caught in some transgression, you who are spiritual should correct that one in a gentle spirit, looking to yourself, so that you also may not be tempted"* (Galatians 6:1).

Allow me to share a few thoughts on this idea of restoration. First, there is a realization that the "man is overtaken," meaning that he has lost all objectivity and awareness that he is caught in a pitiful condition, which is why he is going to need someone outside himself to speak into his situation. Second, if you are going to be about this business of restoration, you must be spiritual yourself. Now, you could take that as an out and reason, *"Well, I'm certainly not spiritual, so I'll let someone else...more spiritual than I am...handle this situation."* That frees us to turn away and do nothing without feeling any guilt, right? Wrong. Not only do we have an obligation to be involved in this ministry of encouragement, we also have a mandate to pursue and deepen our spirituality. Next, I would remind you that the ultimate goal is always restoration. It would be easy for me or anyone to listen to the stories I do every day and enter into a self-justifying arrogant judgmental attitude with the person(s). That is why I have kept a small stone on a table in

THE LITURGY OF MARRIAGE • 129

my office, always within eyeshot for me, to remind me of the words of Jesus, *"Let him who is without sin throw the first stone..."* I am a firm believer in restoration. If not, where would any of us be? As is often aptly said, "There, but for the grace of God, go I." I reserve great hope for every couple I treat, not based in my performance as a counselor, but in the knowledge that the grace of God reaches farther than our sin can plunge us.

And one more comment on Paul's words to us. The Apostle to the world admonishes us to *"look to yourself, lest you too be tempted."* Some of you are no doubt defending against such an implication, that you could fall into such a sin. During one of my clinical courses in graduate school, a guest speaker from the Denver Police Department came and spoke to our class. As I recall, the detective's reason for coming was to talk about the prevalent violence, crime and gang involvement in the area and to help us better understand the psychological profile of a criminal. However, my takeaway was more limited to one statement he made that I can still quote word for word today. *"On any given day, any one of us is capable of doing just about anything!"* *No way!* I retorted in my head. What a stupid thing to even suggest. Those of us who are educated, grounded in the faith, stable in our actions...would never even consider doing the unthinkable. It did not take long for me to discover the life-shattering truth of his words that day and I will never be the same.

I don't write this book just from the vantage point of a marriage and family therapist who sits in the place of perceived wisdom, giving sage counsel to the poor souls caught in their trespasses (or in the tragic consequences of others' trespasses). I write this book as a fellow sinner, well versed in sin, but also saturated in the redemptive and restorative grace of God. My first marriage ended in the heartache of divorce and I have never fully recovered from that failure on my part to God, my wife, our children, and to me. But the memory of my failure also keeps me in a place of humility as I have the sacred honor of entering the pain of people's lives and marriages.

Songs have always played a powerful role in my life, able to move me and inspire me. Do you notice how you can remember the lyrics of a song, but only when you hum or sing the tune? I think that is because of the dual-hemispheric involvement that music provides us, linking the left and right sides of the brain. I have found that to be an excellent therapeutic device as well. Maybe that's why we have the book of Psalms, the song-book of the ancient Israelites. And perhaps that is also why the most repeated command in all of Scripture is *Sing!*

After my failure as a husband and soon after our separation, I would look at the world very differently. I could not understand how everyone else seemed able to go through their lives without the realization that my world was crushing. Christian music ministered to me at that sad time and still does.

With God as my witness, there was one particular song that would inevitably come on the radio at just the right time for me, when I thought I could hang on no longer. The name of the song was *My Redeemer is Faithful and True*⁵. It was so beautifully sung and made famous at the time by a talented singer, Bobby Michaels. Here are the words to the song that still speak so deeply to my bruised spirit:

VERSE ONE

As I look back on the road I've traveled,

I see so many times He carried me through;

And if there's one thing that I've learned in my life,

My Redeemer is faithful and true.

My Redeemer is faithful and true.

CHORUS

My Redeemer is faithful and true.

Everything He has said He will do,

And every morning His mercies are new.

My Redeemer is faithful and true.

VERSE TWO

My heart rejoices when I read the promise

"There is a place I am preparing for you."

I know someday I'll see my Lord face to face,

'Cause my Redeemer is faithful and true.

My Redeemer is faithful and true.

(chorus)

And in every situation He has proved His love to me;

When I lack the understanding, He gives more grace to me.

(chorus)

When the song came on the radio, I literally had to pull the car over and weep like a baby....I still do. A few months later, I learned that the recording artist was coming to a nearby town and giving a concert. I had a front row seat and waited with baited breath for him to sing that song. The rest were good...but that was the only song I came to hear. You know how it is when you hear that first chord and you know exactly what song it is? I heard it. You would have thought someone punched me in the stomach as I wept profusely while those around me sat in bewilderment, probably wondering if I was on medication...or needed to be. After the concert, I approached the stage where he had performed. As an introvert with a fairly strong case of social anxiety, this did not come easily for me, but I had to tell him some of my story and how much his song had ministered to me.

After waiting for what seemed an eternity, I looked face to face at Michaels and told him the whole story in between sighs and tears. Telling my own story of sin and brokenness always bows me down, not in reverence, but in depressing shame. He said my name and I looked up to see this talented and gifted singer who had just so confidently performed for hundreds, now in tears himself. *"Tim, my friend, Steven Curtis Chapman, wrote that song for me when I was going through my own divorce."*

We wept together and held each other through our shared brokenness. People say to me they cannot imagine why I would want to do the work I do, not just treating couples in distress, but also specializing as I do in the treatment of depression and anxiety-related disorders. They have little idea how personal that career decision has been for me.

That word, *brokenness*, has come to mean so much to me. Putting myself through what I did in my own moral failure, brought me invariably to see myself for who I really am—a broken sinner with no hope, save the grace of God. Another of my favorite stories from the Old Testament is that of the call of the prophet Isaiah. Before he was called as a prophet for God, he was a Levitical priest who served in the Temple. One day he was ministering in the Temple, or what we would think of as the Sanctuary, and none other than God Himself showed up to make a grand appearance before Isaiah and call him into the prophetic ministry. Though rather curious given that he was a Priest, Isaiah was shocked out of his mind. A lot of us pray that God would show up in our lives, but we don't usually expect Him to do so. Be careful what you pray, as He just may surprise you.

Isaiah was surprised for sure, and he came to two utter realizations through that experience of the Beatific Vision, also called by theologians a *theophany*, or God-appearance. First, Isaiah saw the Almighty God he served for who He is—a Holy God. The priest fell prostrate before him and declared, what

Scripture scholars call the *trishaggion* (three times holy). We say it every Mass, just before the Lord comes to us in the theophany of the Eucharist. *Holy, Holy, Holy is the Lord of hosts!* I took three years of Hebrew and still love that beautiful language in which the Old Testament was first written. Bear with me as I give you a primer in Hebrew grammar. If you wanted to convey the comparative degree in the English language you would say, for instance, *"That flower is more beautiful than the others,"* or *"He is more generous than his friend."* But if you wanted to convey the superlative in our language, you would say, *"That is the most beautiful flower of all"*, or *"He is the most generous person I have ever met."* But if you were speaking or writing in Hebrew, you would say it quite differently, using repetition to make the distinction. So, the comparative degree for our first example would be—*"That flower is beautiful, beautiful,"* or *"He is generous, generous."* And the superlative in Hebrew would be—*"That is the beautiful, beautiful, beautiful flower!"* or *"He is generous, generous, generous!"*

Okay, you're way ahead of me, aren't you? There is only one description of God that is raised to the third degree in all of Scripture and we find it here in this passage about Isaiah's call to ministry. Our God is *Holy, Holy, Holy!* We should never grow weary of singing this triumphant song to our trinitarian God, as this is the song of the angels gathered around the Throne in the book of Revelation and this will be our song when we too behold Him in all His glory. Isaiah saw the fiery angels, called the seraphim, called such because of their proximity to God, and they were incensing the altar for His presence. Could he have done anything but drop to his knees as he was lifted into the heavenly courts?

Read through the story again. "In the year that King Uzziah died, I saw the Lord sitting on a throne, high and lofty; and the hem of his robe filled the temple. Seraphs were in attendance above him; each had six wings: with two they covered their faces, and with two they covered their feet, and with two they flew. And one called to another and said: 'Holy, holy, holy is the LORD of hosts; the whole earth is full of his glory.' The pivots on the thresholds shook at the voices of those who called, and the house filled with smoke. And I said, 'Woe is me! I am lost, for I am a man of unclean lips, and I live among a people of unclean lips; yet my eyes have seen the King, the LORD of hosts!' Then one of the seraphs flew to me, holding a live coal that had been taken from the altar with a pair of tongs. The seraph touched my mouth with it and said: 'Now that this has touched your lips, your guilt has departed and your sin is blotted out.' Then I heard the voice of the Lord saying, 'Whom shall I send, and who will go for us?' And I said, 'Here am I; send me!' And he said, 'Go...'" (Isaiah 6:1-9, NRSV).

Although I have worked as a therapist over the last quarter of a century, I had opportunities to exercise my ordination as a Protestant pastor, but it became more and more difficult as I studied our Catholic roots in church history. One hurdle was reached during an actual worship service on a Sunday morning at the church where I was preaching on the weekends. Let me set the scene for you. We had a praise band that led the singing on stage, so you would see their instruments and the microphones, music stands and any of the other paraphernalia for having a quality musical experience. We had removed the pulpit, what Catholics would know as the ambo, from the platform and we had a wooden communion table on the floor in front of the steps leading up to the platform. My wife and I were sitting in the front pew, so I would be ready to step up at my cue from the worship leader and start the delivery of my message to the people.

We had just celebrated the Lord's Supper, at least our commemorative version of it with bread and wine, though we often used grape juice (yet another reason to consider the Catholic Church as the one, true Church). The worship team was quietly playing a song of praise and worship and I was feeling especially sensitive to the Holy Spirit. Having been reading the Anglican Book of Common Prayer about liturgical rites of worship, I had this strong compulsion to kneel. After all, we sang songs about kneeling, which was interesting, because we never did really kneel. It was all more than a little platonic, residing more in our heads than our hearts and bodies, where worship is designed to be. Well, here I was, ready to kneel, but I found myself struggling with yet another serious problem. To what or in which direction would I kneel? Do I face the musicians? Do I face the communion table whereupon we had just received the bread and cup? Do I face the beautiful stained-glass window behind the platform? You may laugh, but I was in agony for those few minutes as I tried to weigh out the options. Finally, I just scooted forward in my seat and went down for the plunge, bowing my head and praying, though not without a measure of self-consciousness in the process.

No such confusion exists for us Catholics. We know exactly to whom we should bow and kneel—the Holy One of Israel, the Lamb of God who takes away the sin of the world, the crucified Jesus who is now re-presented to us in the Sacrament of the Eucharist. And we, like Isaiah of old, cry out, *"Holy, holy, holy is the Lord God of hosts!"* Oh that we would all realize fully, or as fully as possible for us, what we are experiencing in this Eucharistic celebration.

Isaiah discovered more in this Temple experience. He came to know who God is in all His holiness, but he also discovered who Isaiah was in all his *un*-holiness. The priest came to the same realization of himself that I had after my failure. And he expresses that realization in the words, *"Woe is me, I am doomed! For I am a man of unclean lips, living among a people of unclean lips, and my eyes have seen the King, the LORD of hosts!"* The first thing that is extremely noteworthy about his statement is the phrase *"Woe is me!"* You see, this phrase was reserved for the pronouncement of judgment, usually given upon a foreign and pagan nation for having denounced the true God or for coming against the people of God. Read through many of the prophets and you will hear them cry out, *"Woe to you, Edom! Woe to you, Moab!"* and then go on to announce a decree of judgment against the nation for their crimes against God and His people. That all makes sense, but what doesn't make sense is that Isaiah is now pronouncing judgment against himself. He is essentially calling down fire and brimstone upon his own head for his sinfulness as an unholy man.

Truthfully, I can understand that response. Someone I love so very much recently said to me, *"You have lived in a purgatory of self-condemnation for years."* That person was right and what is even more sad is that I have so often pronounced a judgment upon myself that the Lord Himself does not even assign to me. I am sitting right now in the hallway of a Catholic Church on the grounds of one of the most spectacular retreat centers I have ever seen, nestled in the foothills of the Pikes Peak region in Colorado Springs. Walking the grounds after lunch, I had to be sure to look up frequently so as not to bump into any of the friendly deer sauntering about the grounds. The most amazing experience was listening to the music of Fernando Ortega sing the song, *Give Me Jesus*—the song that was playing the day my father died in my arms on June 11, 2013. Naturally, Dad was on my mind and I began praying for him in his own pilgrimage to that Beatific Vision of God. As tears filled my eyes, I looked up slightly to see a small sign that read—"Sacred Place." It was a small cemetery with the graves of some of the sisters who had been buried in this special ground. And then I saw a deer lying by one of the grave markers, curled up like my golden retriever, eyes looking at me as if to say to me, *"Your Dad is in a good place."* That is a gift from God, my friend.

I am waiting in this hallway for the priest with whom I am to meet for spiritual direction. He is late and may have forgotten. How we must pray for these overly taxed men who lead us in our faith and minister to us in our pain and sin. But what I am aware of is that it is pitch black in this hallway where I sit alone and type out these words. If I stand up and move, the motion detectors signal the lights to come on, but if I return to my chair and remain seated, I am again left in the darkness. Not to overly spiritualize, but that is all too characteristic of how I've lived my life since my own personal "original sin"—living in a darkness of self-condemnation, rather than moving into the light of His unimaginable grace and mercy.

The next observation I would offer from Isaiah's response is his statement—*"For I am lost"* or sometimes translated as—*"For I am ruined."* The term used in the original Hebrew of the text denotes almost a sort of psychiatric breakdown for the man in which he is mentally, emotionally, spiritually shattered by the overwhelming epiphany he has just witnessed and what he has learned of God and of himself. This, too, is a good thing for us to experience—the brokenness that is evident in our lives, despite the pretense that we have it all together. Some even have deluded themselves into the belief that they are not too bad and don't need quite as much grace as the next person whose life is more obviously sinful.

Finally, Isaiah acknowledges his uncleanness in the manifestation of his speech, saying he is a man of *"unclean lips."* To use the vernacular, we might say Isaiah had a "dirty mouth." Jesus had something to say about the defilement of a man's lips also, stating, *"It is not what enters one's mouth that defiles that person; but what comes out of the mouth is what defiles one"* (Matthew 15:11).

Thankfully, the story does not end on that note. We are told that one of the seraphim took a burning coal from the altar, touched the mouth of Isaiah and said the words of absolution from God—*"'See,' he said, 'now that this has touched your lips, your wickedness is removed, your sin purged.'"* Surely I am not the only one who is indescribably moved when I hear the words of absolution from the priest after a good confession has been offered. Then Isaiah hears the Lord say, *"Whom shall I send? Who will go for us?"* And the cleansed prophet is now ready to begin his new ministry and responds saying, *"Here am I! Send me."* Take note the grammatical structure of those words—"Here am I." the phrase in the Hebrew connotes not a geographical location of where he is, but a description of his readiness of spirit.

Like Moses, who needed forty years in the desert to polish his ego down to a usable size—even to a point where the one who had been raised in Pharaoh's court had absolutely no confidence in himself and then, and only then, was Moses considered ready and fit for ministry—so it was with Isaiah. And so it is with all of us. God cares little about our pedigrees, our accomplishments, even our talents and ambitions that may be in His own name. What He does care about is that a person knows he is weak and helpless to do anything that counts for anything, without the sustaining, all-sufficient grace of God. St. Paul came to know this and said as much, *"If I must boast, I will boast of the things that show my weakness...because of the abundance of the revelations. Therefore, that I might not become too elated, a thorn in the flesh was given to me, an angel of Satan, to beat me, to keep me from being too elated. Three times I begged the Lord about this, that it might leave me, but he said to me, 'My grace is sufficient for you, for power is made perfect in weakness.' I will rather boast most gladly of my weaknesses, in order that the power of Christ may dwell with me"* (2 Corinthians 11:30; 12:7-10).

Remember the story of Adam and Eve in the creation narrative we talked about earlier? After their transgression of distrust and disobedience, *"the man and woman hid themselves from the LORD God among the trees of the garden. The LORD God then called to the man and asked him: 'Where are you?'"* (Genesis 3:8-9). God had not lost sight of where the man had wandered off to in the garden, nor was He ignorant of what the man had done. You see, the question was not for God's sake, but for the man's sake. *"Where are you, Adam? Do you know what you have done? Can you take full responsibility for your failure?"* But Adam could not and so we are told he hid himself, saying to God, *"I was afraid."* This is what sin does to us, but even more, this is what the hiding of our sin does to us—it drowns us in terrifying and paralyzing fear. God is dying (or should we say he has died?) to forgive you out of His magnanimous love for you, and too often we cower behind the tree in fear instead of exposing our weakness and shame so that He might touch our wound with the burning embers, cleanse us thoroughly and then use us powerfully in ministry for His sake.

Keith and Allison's Story

It is not the adultery that will destroy a marriage—it is the deception that kills. Keith and Allison's story helps to demonstrate this truth. Allison knew it was wrong and even knew firsthand the pain that befalls a spouse, a marriage and a family when there is marital betrayal, having lived through her own father's crisis that brought about her parents' divorce. Struggling since childhood to feel worthwhile and loved, the ghosts of her past family experiences and losses haunted her, making her vulnerable to any man who would prey upon her weakness. The slide from friendship to inappropriate disclosure to the affair happened over months, but Allison finally ended it, swearing never to tell a soul, especially not Keith. Fear is a monster that holds its own prey captive and it fed on Allison's inner peace, leaving her anxious, depressed, and wracked with guilt and shame at the thought that her secret might ever be discovered. Converting to the Catholic Church would not necessarily help with the problem, given the requirement to go to Confession. That was *not* what she needed, or so she reasoned to herself.

Like a malignant cancer, her guilt and fear wove together within her to feed a frenzy of anxiety and a depth of depression from which no medication or treatment could provide relief. Providing couples a place to tell each other the truth is a constant effort in my work. When it happens, there is such an outpouring of freedom and relief for both parties. For Allison, however, it was not a professional counselor who would unlock the door to her fear and compel her to extricate the monstrous lie within her that had been feeding on her peace all those years. It was another woman who would set her free from her self-made prison. Mary, the Blessed Mother, to whom Allison eventually consecrated herself, would be the instrument of healing for this pained soul. Never take lightly our Catholic faith. Allison had little idea that making a 33-day journey of commitment to the Mother of our Lord would lead her to open up with Keith and tell him the whole agonizing truth of how she had betrayed him in their marriage.

Have you ever stared at an artist's masterpiece work, attended the opening night of a famous show, watched a drama of suspense unfold or just been caught up in a moment of ecstasy? This is only a hint of what it feels to be in the presence of forgiveness between two lovers, a dance of grace. It doesn't happen immediately, nor should it, as the pain must be felt and the offense appreciated for what it was. A counselor can see signs of it coming and you watch in anticipation. Allison's disclosure and Keith's initial response of anger and rejection, what she feared most, pushed her beyond what she could handle. A hospital where she could find rest, treatment, support and solace would be necessary for a time.

Being a devout Catholic and a product of a broken home, it did not take long for Keith to hear the voice of God speaking to him, coaching him to forgive. He all but begged me to take him to see Allison in the hospital. I stood at the door of her room and watched the scene. It was as if the camera slowed as he walked toward her and sat on the bed beside her, gazing into her eyes, ministering the gift that only he could give— forgiveness. Grace is a medicine that heals the soul, and it is a miracle to witness the performance of that healing. Every part of that movement is forever etched in my mind and heart.

Attending a Retrouvaille weekend was just the "treatment" they needed to bring healing and restoration to their marriage. How fitting that less than two months later they would discover Allison was bearing their fourth child. Who knows...if it's a girl, maybe they should name her *Grace*. One more note about the healing and restoration process. As a professional marriage counselor, I advocate for seeking the help of a qualified provider, but I also want to give a strong word of endorsement for other methods, groups, and means of working through one's problems and finding help for your marriage. Retrouvaille is just one of those excellent alternatives that couples should explore and consider.

Bringing It Home

Detours are part of life, at least most of our lives. Unlike the good Dr. Foster we are more than likely living out a journey unlike the one we may have mapped out for ourselves so many years ago. Have you ever considered what your "Eden" looked like in your imagination back then before you entered marriage? It was probably filled with dreams, expectations and lots of joy. The reality of your marriage has likely been marked by numerous disappointments, struggles and even pain at times. Yet as St. John Paul II encouraged, that *echo of Eden* remains in our souls.

THE OLD TESTAMENT

1. If your dating and courtship period of your relationship constituted more of an *Eden-like* phase, contemplate the times when you realized you were living *outside the Garden* in your marriage? How did that disillusion you about your marriage and your spouse?

2. In the section on "Menu Catholics," could you see yourself at all? What parts of our Catholic faith and the clear

teachings of the Catholic Church have you found difficult to follow, especially in your marriage?

3. Hopefully infidelity has never threatened your marriage relationship. If, however, you have known the sad pain that accompanies unfaithfulness, how did it change you, your partner, and your relationship? If you have never known such a threat, what are you doing to prevent that unfortunate temptation from ever befalling your marriage?

TRY THIS EXERCISE

Fidelity is more than just not having sexual relations with anyone outside of marriage. Every couple needs to talk through what is acceptable and unacceptable to them. For instance, is it okay to have lunch with someone of the opposite gender? What about supper? Drinks? Should you share anything personal about your marriage relationship with someone else before asking your partner's permission? You get the idea. These are not clear-cut, nor are they universal. You should think carefully through the principles and guidelines you would like to have for your marriage that will protect it from the threats this world brings.

Another critical area where a serious conversation needs to take place in every marriage is around technology and social media. From texting to emails to social media websites where people share some of the most exposing and personal information, these are breeding grounds for illicit interaction to take place. Don't let this dimension of your lives go without direct attention. So this is your exercise for the week. Develop your own set of guidelines that will serve to boundary your marriage from any threats to fidelity and keep it looking like a shining example of grace!

CHAPTER FIVE

The Psalms
*Orientation, Disorientation
and a New Orientation*

St. Augustine put it well when he said, *"He who sings, prays twice."* I certainly have no claim to any fame, but it has been my privilege to know some singers who did become well known in the music industry. One of them is Rich Mullins, a songwriter, singer and teacher. You may be familiar with some of his music, perhaps his most well-known song, *Awesome God*[6]. The chorus is triumphant, extolling the magnificent power resident in our Holy God:

Our God is an awesome God, He reigns from heaven above

With wisdom, power, and love, Our God is an awesome God.

Rich and I attended the same undergraduate Christian university in Cincinnati back in the 70s. Although he was in the same class and roomed across the hall my first year, we were not close, but I had a curiosity about him that grew over the months and years. Unashamedly brash in his manner with most everyone, including his professors, he had some understandable challenges getting through the program. Little did we know how talented, gifted and full of the Spirit he was. Those gifts found expression over the next twenty years and gave incredible inspiration to believers across all denominational lines. His music and his life have touched mine seriously, giving me inspiration, as well as the challenge to step out in faith to do what God has called me to do. For me, this book is one of those major steps. I'll talk more about Rich when we get to the section on the Creed, but I just want to point you to his music as a wonderful example of Christian praise music that can play a part in helping you create a climate of praise in your marriage, family and home.

Rich's closest friends and many of his admirers aren't comfortable hearing that he had a strong affinity and a never-ending thirst to better understand the Roman Catholic Church. I have it on good testimony that he was planning to enter the Church on the Feast Day of St. Francis, Saturday, October 4th, 1997. Rich was killed in a tragic auto accident two weeks earlier on the evening of Friday, September 19th, 1997. Talk to his Protestant Evangelical friends and they will either deny it or tell you that may have been why the Lord took him when he did. A few of us have a different slant on the story. His movement toward Catholicism was costing him greatly, not just financially (Rich never cared much about that anyway, having taken the Franciscan vow of poverty and giving most of his earnings to a foundation for Native Americans), but he felt the grief of what is involved when a prominent evangelical crosses over the Tiber into Rome to be part of the one, holy, catholic and apostolic Church. Perhaps then, God wanted Rich to receive his First Eucharist in the heavenly sanctuary.

The most respected contemporary Scripture scholar on the Psalms is Walter Brueggemann. His work is not for the timid, but if you have a desire to understand the Old Testament and especially the Psalms, spend a few dollars on one of his many books. In his work, *Praying the Psalms*, he beautifully portrays a simple scheme for viewing these life songs. Brueggemann writes, *"I suggest...that our life of faith consists in moving with God in terms of: (a) being securely oriented; (b) being painfully disoriented; and (c) being surprisingly reoriented."*[7] Take a few moments to ponder that three-part scenario to see if you can find it to be true in your life. These ancient lyrics that would have been set to tune in the liturgy of the Israelites, were deeply intertwined with the people's lived experience. That is still true for us. Try this some morning—open your daily newspaper or internet page where you can get the news of the previous day. Then turn to one of the psalms and randomly pick one to read. Now, after reading the news story and the Psalm, look to see if there might be any connections. My hunch is that you will find at least one. The transcendent nature of the

Psalms means it is not tied down to certain historical events and circumstances, but is able to speak into our 21st century life circumstances and marriages.

Marriage can be described as a sacramental symphony with three movements, yet too few couples ever discover all three. The first stage is Enchantment, which is what we were describing when we talked about how a relationship begins and grows, all leading up to the decision to marry, if they so choose. Couples enjoy a delightful time in the development of their love when they feel so dearly the feelings of infatuation, affection and attraction. These feelings are like pre-marital aphrodisiacs that will build desire for closeness between the partners. Don't forget what we said about how couples in loving relationships are healthier, evidenced particularly by their heightened immune system to fight against infections and such ailments. Developing and restoring romantic love in your marriage relationship can be good for your medical health. *"Forget the Yoga honey; let's snuggle!"*

The second movement of marriage is Disenchantment and it is about as far in the other direction from the first stage as you can systemically move. It can begin as early as the wedding night. The partners begin to see each other through the lenses of everyday life. Made up faces are replaced with no makeup and morning breath. Well-planned dates are replaced with excursions to Walmart. Romance is replaced with the rat-race of the demands of career, houses, money, children and so much more. Amid all these demands and stressors, the couple's relationship slides into the minor key of disenchantment, leaving them with a mutual and growing dissatisfaction.

Finally, and hopefully, the couple works their way through to the final movement of a marriage—Maturity. At this stage, they have discovered the truth of what we're talking about in these pages, but even more, they have learned how to receive and live out of the sacramental graces given to us in marriage. Married partners have access to special graces and blessings not available to those outside the vocation of marriage. This may sound discriminatory to some, perhaps working under the assumption that God owes everyone the same number, form and degree of blessing. Nothing could be further from the truth. God owes us nothing. Jews who truly observe the Passover Seder know this to be true. About 1000 years ago, rabbis added a song to the ancient feast known as the *Dayenu*. It is usually sung during the observance and recounts the many ways God has blessed us, prefacing each blessing with the word—"dayenu", which is translated—*It would have been enough!* Listen to some of the words:

If He had brought us out from Egypt, and had not carried out judgments against them Dayenu, it would have been enough.

If He had carried out judgments against them, and not against their idols Dayenu, it would have been enough.

If He had split the sea for us, and had not taken us through it on dry land Dayenu, it would have been enough.

If He had taken us through the sea on dry land, and had not drowned our oppressors in it Dayenu, it would have been enough.

If He had fed us the manna, and had not given us the Shabbat Dayenu, it would have been enough.[8]

Isn't that a uniquely godly way of looking at our lives and what God is doing in our lives? Too often we find ourselves in a very different frame of mind, with more of a "not-Dayenu" worldview that might go something like this:

She was so nice before we were married, but now she seems so selfish not-Dayenu, it just is not enough.

He treated me like a princess before we were married, but now he only cares about his work not-Dayenu, it just is not enough.

We bought this big house, but now we can't afford to go out on those expensive dates and vacations, not-Dayenu, it just is not enough.

We have three children, but they're driving us crazy with their wants and needs not-Dayenu, it just is not enough.

We used to be so much in love, but everything changed and now we're not sure we should stay together not-Dayenu, it just is not enough.

A mature marriage is known by the spirit of gratitude, from which it exudes. Mature couples don't operate under the childlike notion that nothing changes and everything is constant. They are smart enough to realize how challenging life can be; they work together to find and develop the resources to meet the challenges together and by the grace of the Lord. Let me again pull out my very broad stroke brush and offer a comment about our contemporary American culture—*Many of us work under a not-so-subtle misconception that this world is supposed to give us everything we need to keep us happy, comfortable and healthy.* That fundamental assumption about life will open the door to untold disappointments, resentments and maybe even an all-out rejection of God. Why? Because in this world, outside the gates of Eden, we are not promised happiness, comfort and health, at least not as a constant reality. For some of you that may ring of blasphemy, but for others, you have come to know the truth of that statement.

One couple is drowning in anger over their flooded basement in the new five-bedroom home they just built six months ago. Another couple is flooded with tears of joy that their newborn infant with *spina bifida* could come home from the intensive care unit of the hospital last week. One husband bemoans being passed over for the third time as a senior partner in his law firm—another man rejoices that he landed a job in facility management after being laid off six months ago from his position as lead engineer with his company. One wife complains incessantly that her husband needs to get out of the house more and stop being so "co-dependent" on her. Another wife counts her blessings for their seventeen years of marriage as she grieves his death from an accident. Would you help me write a sort of Christian Dayenu for marriage? I'll get it started and you finish it, personalizing it for your own marriage.

If He had brought us together all those years ago and only given us days to share our love Dayenu, it would have been enough.

If He had given us the past _____ years together but not a day more Dayenu, it would have been enough.

If He had given us a roof over our heads and food to feed our family but not the home of our dreams with loads of cash leftover Dayenu, it would have been enough.

If He had given us our children to love and raise in godliness but not the guarantee they would get the academic and athletic scholarships to fund their education to be successful giants in their field Dayenu, it would have been enough.

And if He had given me a moment to cherish my spouse's love and look within her soul to see the pain of her life but not provided the way to stop all the hurt and give her heaven right now so that I could just be with her in contentment to enjoy His graces Dayenu, it would have been enough.

Bringing It Home

The cycle of orientation-disorientation-reorientation described in this chapter can be used to describe anyone's life at some time or another. In all likelihood you have already been there and maybe found your way back to solid ground. If not, and you still feel the agony of disorientation, then I pray you will see the light of transformation coming soon. If you have come to know that place of new-found stability, then become a source of encouragement to those around you and help them patiently rediscover the hope of something better.

THE PSALMS

1. With a transparent openness, share with your spouse a time of personal disorientation where your faith was shaken. Encourage your partner to probe and explore with questions to better understand the pain of that part of your life.

2. Enchantment, Disenchantment, and Maturity. In which season do you consider your own marriage to be? Discuss why you think it to be where it is and, if not at the third

level, what it would take to move it further along toward maturity.

3. Ask yourself a serious question and give yourself an honest response. Are you a thankful person? Think about it.

TRY THIS EXERCISE

Dayenu! You probably expected this exercise. I want the two of you to write out your own *Marriage Dayenu*. Use the phrase—*If He had...it would have been enough.* Finish that comment of gratitude as many times as you can. Exhaust yourselves with memories of thankfulness and then close out the time in prayer together. Over the coming weeks, choose one day when you will recite the Dayenu together for the next seven weeks. Pray for a spirit of gratitude to overwhelm your life and watch what happens.

If you prefer, you might be creative and write your own *psalm* of praise or thanksgiving or choose your favorite Psalm from the Scriptures, memorize it and maybe even print it out for a frame on your wall.

CHAPTER SIX

The New Testament Letters
Written with You In Mind

During the Sunday Mass, following the responsorial psalm, we sometimes hear a reading from one of the New Testament letters, usually written by Saint Paul, the author of more than two-thirds of the New Testament, Saint Peter, Saint Luke or Saint John. Critics of the Bible will discount the words of Scripture by confining them to a historical context that has little or no application to this modern world. And while that is true to a point and the context must be taken into consideration in making a good interpretation of the text, it is also possible to take the point too far. The consequence of doing so is that much of the teaching on subjects like marriage, sexuality or any other relevant controversial topic are dismissed as much too ancient and biased by the sociological setting to have any meaning for this sophisticated day and so highly educated age.

Take as an example a statement from 2 Corinthians—*"For I am jealous of you with the jealousy of God, since I betrothed you to one husband to present you as a chaste virgin to Christ"* (11:2). Frequently, an analogy of marriage is used in the Bible for the relationship between God and his people. He is the groom and we, His people, are His bride. In fact, the Old Testament prophets took the imagery so far as to accuse the people of Israel of committing spiritual adultery in their blended worship of the pagan gods with the true worship of the one true God. And now St. Paul makes what seems an absurd comment about God's jealousy for us, wanting us to be presented in our *marriage* to Him *"as a chaste virgin."* Is he really serious in his suggestion that people hold off on having sexual intimacy until the marriage? How archaic and unrealistic!

Or what of the words of the author of Hebrews—*"Let marriage be held in honor by all, and let the marriage bed be kept undefiled; for God will judge fornicators and adulterers"* (13:4)? That verse is replete with problems. First, to say that we should honor marriage is comparable to saying we should not honor other close relationships that are promoted in our society as being marriage. And what does the author mean about the "marriage bed" being "kept undefiled"? Surely he isn't telling us to be faithful and maintain fidelity in marriage. Has he not read anything about having an "open marriage" as was prominently pushed in the 60s? And finally, how audacious to talk about judgment for "fornicators and adulterers". In this age of tolerance, we should have nothing of that kind of adamancy.

Marriages are sorely in need of words of exhortation that would give instruction and a model for their relationship. The absence of well-grounded principles for relationships leave couples at the mercy of their past and their emotions to determine and measure their relationship. The writings of the New Testament are as much as anything a book of ethical conduct, showing us how to practice the faith purchased for us by our Lord and delivered to us by the Apostles. But as much as we need to hear the readings of the early Church, we also are in desperate need of examples living out this ethos of life in the home. I like to inquire of couples about their own models of marriage. Think of some couples in your life who have set the stage for what you hope your own marriage to be. What are they like? How do they communicate? When they argue how do they get through it? Then I ask them to think of some couples whose marriages are utter disasters they would never want to emulate. How do they communicate? What's different about these two kinds of couples?

My past life in the Protestant evangelical world exposed me to quite a variety of worship styles and services. The most common element of these faith-filled communities was their emphasis on the preaching of the New Testament in a way that was extremely practical. The "how to" sermon was the most typically heard in a church service. You could be certain you would hear a twenty-to-thirty-minute message, usually with a fill-in-the-blank handout, on some relevant life issue giving you a biblically-based series of steps and principles for living out the faith of New Testament Christianity. Now that I've been in the Catholic Church for the past twelve years I will have to say that I have become accustomed to the nine-minute homily, but I can also admit that I usually long for more. My mind and heart need to hear more frequent admonishment for proper godly living. Nowhere is the need greater than in the context of the marriage and family.

I came across a book in graduate school years ago entitled something like *Spirit-Filled Family Living*. My recollection is that the volume was not all that impressive but the core thesis was striking. The author laid out the premise that if you really want to see spiritual living you will have to look at the home life of the person. You see anyone can pull off the practice in front of the crowd. It's in the flesh-and-blood arena of people grinding through their daily tasks, making a living, paying bills, raising children, and every other stress-producing activity that we discover the limitations of our spirituality.

Probably the most contested passages of the New Testament about marriage are those dreadful words of Paul, wherein he speaks of the man as the "head of the home" and gives encouragement to the wife to "submit to the man." Could anything be any more dated than such words of first-century chauvinism? Or so we often think. Yet a proper understanding

THE LITURGY OF MARRIAGE • 163

of the text will reveal a view of male headship that mirrors the servant role of Christ Himself as He sacrificially gave Himself up for His bride, the Church. And we need look no further than our Blessed Mother to discover the epitome of spousal love as she submits to the will of God. A proper reading of the text recognizes that submission is always and ultimately to the Lord, whether husband or wife.

Leadership in the home is such a confusing concept in our day. The pendulum from dictatorial dominance to passive retreat has left us questioning the viability of any element of the apostle's recommendations of how to live as man and wife. I prefer to see it as a dance in which the partners move to the tempo of the Spirit, requiring them to study each other deeply and practice faithfully the moves of servanthood, humility, tenderness and compassion. We should not allow the problem of not yet being an accomplished dancer to lead us to think it is not possible to achieve this beautiful dream. Like any other dream, it will require dedication, practice and strong motivation to reach. In the end, it will be worth it all.

The most beautiful passage heard most frequently in the marriage ceremony comes from Paul's words to the Corinthians in what is often depicted as the love chapter of the Bible, I Corinthians 13. You'll recognize the words. "Love is patient. Love is kind." If you want a good examination of conscience around your relationship with your wife or husband try taking out the word love from the verses and replace it with your own name. If it sounds a bit dissonant you may want to take that as a conviction to work harder in that area of your faith.

> "If I speak in human and angelic tongues but do not have love, I am a resounding gong or a clashing cymbal. And if I have the gift of prophecy and comprehend all mysteries and all knowledge; if I have all faith so as to move mountains but do not have love, I am nothing. If I give away everything I own, and if I hand my body over so that I may boast but do not have love, I gain nothing. Love is patient, love is kind. It is not jealous, is not pompous, it is not inflated, it is not rude, it does not seek its own interests, it is not quick-tempered, it does not brood over injury, it does not rejoice over wrongdoing but rejoices with the truth. It bears all things, believes all things, hopes all things, endures all things. Love never fails." (I Corinthians 13:1-8)

But the ultimate consideration in the New Testament is when heaven is recognized as a triumphal, long-awaited marriage ceremony. *"Then the angel said to me, 'Write this: Blessed are those who have been called to the wedding feast of the Lamb.' And he said to me, 'These words are true; they come from God.'"* (Revelation 19:9). The Holy Spirit gives us a depiction of marriage as the ultimate relationship that mirrors the glory of the Lord. Just as we tried to illustrate in the Gloria, a godly marriage is a relationship that looks like God in His trinitarian, other-centered love that compels us to come to Him.

Let me draw this section on the liturgy of the Word and its relevance for marriage to a conclusion with this helpful exchange. Protestants don't have a Pope, but they do have Billy Graham, the long-time evangelist who held his crusades in nearly every major city across the country for decades. I came across a reprint of one of his syndicated columns recently.

DEAR DR. GRAHAM: I know I ought to read my Bible, but every time I try to read it, I just end up getting confused. I never was a very good student, and all those strange names and places in the Old Testament get me lost. Is the Bible really that important? What am I doing wrong?

Mrs. L.Y.

DEAR MRS. L.Y.: I notice you are married; did you ever get a letter from your husband-to-be and decide you wouldn't bother reading it because his handwriting was poor, or you were too busy or for some other reason? I doubt it. And yet that's what many of us do with the Bible. The Bible is God's "love letter" to us, telling us not only that He loves us, but showing what He has done to demonstrate His love. It also tells us how we should live, because God knows what is best for us and He wants us to experience it. Never forget: The Bible is God's Word, given to us so we can know and follow Him. Let me suggest first of all that you begin with one of the Gospels. Christ is the center of the Bible, and the Gospels tell us about His life and teachings. In other words, don't start at the beginning of the Bible but at its center—with Jesus Christ.[9]

Catholics, on the other hand, do have a Pope who speaks wisdom into our life circumstances. The Holy Father, Francis, has offered the Church such a teaching in the 2016 Post-

Synodal Apostolic Exhortation *Amoris Laetitia*[10], a letter address to bishops, priests and deacons, consecrated persons, Christian married couples, and all the lay faithful on love in the family. I strongly encourage you to take the time to read this beautiful treatise filled with rich theology and practical encouragement for marriage and family life.

Bringing It Home

Is it difficult for you to embrace the words of St. Paul and the other authors of the readings from the New Testament we hear each weekend during the Mass? Well, you are probably not alone if you answered in the affirmative. Not only are they difficult to interpret and understand in our modern day and culture, they are equally challenging to carry out on a regular basis. Talk of sacrifice and submission is not altogether popular these days. We are being called to a powerfully unique and distinctive quality of marriage. None of us can do it in our own strength, only by the mercy of God.

THE NEW TESTAMENT LETTERS

1. What is at least one practice you find yourself doing in your marriage that emulates what you saw modeled in your parents' marriage? Is it a good practice or one you might need to modify or even eliminate? Talk through this together.

2. If you could request one *How-to?* homily from your priest what would it be?

3. For husbands, what does *servant leadership* mean to you and how have you done at living it out with your wife? For wives, what does Marian-like submission mean to you and how have you done at living it out with your husband and with God?

TRY THIS EXERCISE

This exercise will require a little extra effort on your part. Go online or locate a Strong's Exhaustive Concordance of the Bible and look up the word *marriage*. Do a bit of a study on the word and how it is used in the Bible. Write down what you learn as you look up the various Scripture verses and then think about how well you are doing in practicing the type of relational behavior described or prescribed in those passages. Identify at least three behaviors you will begin to change as a result of your investigation

EXAMPLES:

    Hebrews 13:1-8

    Ephesians 5:21-33

    1 Corinthians 6:12-20

    1 Corinthians 7:1-7

    Romans 7:1-6

CHAPTER SEVEN

The Gospels
What would Jesus do?

D o you recall that movement that spread in the 90s, in which some well-intentioned marketing-oriented believers thought it might be a great way to get people to be more Christlike, not to mention to sell quite a few rubber bracelets, if we could just stop and ask ourselves one question when we are confused and uncertain what to do or what decision to make. The question was simple, but very hard at the same time—*What would Jesus do?* It was promoted as the easiest way to live out our Christian faith. The proponents are probably right but, as I said, the simplistic nature of the admonition is countered by the difficulty of knowing how our Lord would respond to life situations we face or the decisions we must make at this place in history.

Furthermore, with this being a book about marriage everyone knows, except perhaps the author of that fictitious *Da Vinci Code* book, that Jesus wasn't married. If our Lord was never married, how can we know what He would do in the context of our marriages? It's a fair question, yet founded on some problematic assumptions. It assumes that Christ has no capacity to speak into our lives if He has not experienced the life we live. That's like saying you have no right to caution our children on their misbehavior, unless you yourself have misbehaved accordingly. Maybe you have misbehaved, and you can use the wisdom you gained from having experienced the consequences of that behavior, but if you have not had the experience it does not negate the truth of the potential consequences. What is more, we are told in the book of Hebrews regarding Jesus, our high priest—*"For we do not have a high priest who is unable to sympathize with our weaknesses, but we have one who in every respect has been tested as we are, yet without sin"* (4:15).

The author is clearly informing us that Jesus is very much able to be sympathetic with what we go through. Someone does not need to have had every experience that brought about pain to be able to have valid sympathy for all pain. Think about the pain you've felt in your past or maybe right now. Perhaps it is physical pain or maybe emotional, or even the combination of the two with added spiritual pain and suffering. Jesus knows that pain, not just because He endured it on the cross, but because He endures it for us right now. In the apocalyptic writing of St. John, he depicts our Lord, Jesus Christ, as a slain Lamb standing amid the throne (Revelation 5:6). And the Hebrews writer goes on to encourage us— *"Let us therefore approach the throne of grace with boldness, so that we may receive mercy and find grace to help in time of need"* (4:16).

Let's give more practical consideration to the question of what Jesus would do in any of the kinds of situations we face in our marriages. Why don't you sit down with your spouse and spend a few minutes thinking about how you think Jesus Christ would respond?

Scenario One – Your spouse has been under enormous pressure with her job and lately has been irritable and impatient. On this occasion, you ask her to help you with the dishes and she snaps at you, saying— *"Can you not give me a break? I'm exhausted and now you want me to help you do something as menial as clean up a few plates? You are so selfish!"*

What would Jesus do?

Scenario Two – Your spouse has just learned his father received a diagnosis of cancer and may not survive even to the holidays in three months. He doesn't want to talk about it and changes the subject when you try to bring it up.

What would Jesus do?

Scenario Three – You discovered your spouse has been texting a friend of the opposite gender and, after looking through some of the texts, you're worried she may be getting emotionally or even physically attached to him.

What would Jesus do?

Scenario Four – You're feeling distant from your partner, even starting to wonder if your marriage will survive the gap.

What is worse, you find yourself focusing on his negative traits and behaviors, sensing a growing negative attitude toward him. You worry that you aren't thinking clearly, but can't help comparing him to other men who seem to be much more attentive to their wives—better husbands in more ways than you can count.

What would Jesus do?

The Gospel books of Matthew, Mark, Luke and John contain the testimony of the Apostles' experience of the life of Jesus Christ. Each is written with a slightly different purpose to a different audience and providing us a different perspective of our Lord's life and ministry. By attending Mass each Sunday, we read through the important themes and sections of all four accounts. During the season of Easter, the Church takes the Gospel readings from John for all three years of the lectionary. But I would highly recommend that you plan to read through the four books of the Gospels as a couple regularly as well. The lessons, particularly the ones on how to live the Christian life, are powerful in these books. Where better to apply that ethical guide than in the home with our spouse and children?

Another suggestion for you as you read through the Gospels is to personalize the messages you encounter in the text. My wife and son usually roll their eyes at me when I play a silly game, that maybe isn't all that silly, during our times of reading through the daily lectionary readings together. I will frequently insert each of their names in an attempt to both engage them in the narrative and have some fun.

Now, on a little more serious note, you can do another form of this on your own that I find very convicting. This is also a way to personalize the Scriptures by inserting your own name in the text. Let me illustrate for you by taking a section from one of my favorite portions of the Gospel of John, in chapter 15:

> "This is my commandment: love one another, (Tim), as I love you. No one has greater love than this, to lay down (your) life for your friends. You are my friend if you do what I command you. I no longer call you a slave (Tim), because a slave does not know what the master is doing. I have called you (my) friend, (Tim), because I have told you everything I have heard from my Father. (Tim), it was not you who chose me, but I who chose you and appointed you to go and bear fruit that will remain, so that whatever you ask the Father in my name he may give you. This I command you: love one another (in your marriage)" (vv.12-17).

In this beautifully poignant passage, Jesus implores us to love, and how significant and pertinent is that admonition within our marriages. Not only did our Lord choose you to love and bear fruit, but He has chosen your spouse. Remember that the next time you are tempted to be rude or unkind. To treat your life partner in such a way is to treat someone who has been chosen of Christ in such a manner. Recall also the words of Jesus, *"Amen, I say to you, whatever you did for one of these least brothers of mine, you did for me"* (Matthew 25:40).

What those words teach us is that your spouse is Jesus! C.S. Lewis said, *"...the Church exists for nothing else but to draw men into Christ, to make them little Christs."* The term *Christ* is the Greek translation of the Hebrew word *messiah*, meaning "Anointed One," just as the kings of Israel were known as *messiah's* anointed to reign over the kingdom at the time of their own "baptism" with oil (cf. I Samuel 10:1; 16:13). Listen to the words from the Catechism of the Catholic Church:

> "Baptism not only purifies from all sins, but also makes the neophyte "a new creature," an adopted son of God, who has become a "partaker of the divine nature," member of Christ and co-heir with him, and a temple of the Holy Spirit" (CCC 1265).

> "By Baptism they share in the priesthood of Christ, in his prophetic and royal mission. They are "a chosen race, a royal priesthood, a holy nation, God's own people, that [they] may declare the wonderful deeds of him who called [them] out of darkness into his marvelous light." (CCC 1268)

Before we move on from the Gospels let me make one more observation about the application of the truths of Jesus. Imitating the very Son of God is a daunting task, to say the least. After all, He is God and that seems to give Him at best a bit of an edge on the rest of us. And so, we resign ourselves to never being able to pull off the impossible and rest in our failures. Consider then a more realistic example of sanctity. Look at the Mother of our Lord, the spouse of the Holy Spirit. She gives to us an example of marital love we can better identify with and replicate. Perhaps we should change the question to *What would Mary do?* She would invariably say *yes* to holiness. She would serve with grace, forgive with mercy, love with extravagance. Mary is our model for marriage. Live as she lived and you will harvest the fruit of the Spirit.

Bringing It Home

One priest I enjoy listening to on the radio likes to encourage us to think more in terms of the question—*What would Mary do?* He recommends this since Mary represents the best of humanity and, given that Jesus is God and Man, it might be easier for us to follow the example of our Blessed Mother than that of our Beloved Lord Jesus Christ. Regardless, the admonition is clear and true for each of us to live holy lives unto the Lord.

THE GOSPELS

1. You are awakened in the middle of the night from the dead of sleep. As you wipe the sleep from your eyes you think your mind to be playing tricks on you, but the image in front of you does not fade. It is Jesus and he has come to tell you something very personal. He is about to answer the question most dear to your heart. Listen. What does He say to you? Can you receive it? Will you believe it?

2. Now, in that same appearance, Jesus is going to give you a message for your spouse. A very personal message he/she is dying to hear. What does He say to you? Believe that this

is indeed a word from the Lord and share it with your partner.

3. How does your spouse demonstrate the person of Jesus or Mary in his or her life? Tell him. Tell her. Now.

TRY THIS EXERCISE

This exercise requires you to spend some time in prayerful meditation with the Lord. In fact, you may want to pray a rosary before you even begin. Now take out a piece of paper and a pen. Do it the old-fashioned way. Think of yourself as what those in the first century would call an *amanuensis*—a sort of secretary for St. Paul or one of the other authors of the letters or gospels in the New Testament. Consider that God is going to use you to write a letter directly to your partner from Him. It will be a message that is most meaningful and most personally applicable to the needs, hurts, and lived experience of your spouse. Write it out. Now plan a special time to share your letters with each other. Soak in the moments of divine love.

CHAPTER EIGHT

The Homily at Home
The Domestic Church

In the celebration of the Mass, this is the point where the priest would deliver his homily. I do get a kick out of how Catholics seem to insist it be under fifteen minutes—even 10 would be preferable. They shriek when I tell them I used to preach for thirty to forty minutes on average in my former days as an Evangelical pastor. Remember what we said earlier— Protestant worship services will usually be comprised of a loose arrangement of praise music, prayers (conversational), maybe communion, and the sermon. The format seems to build to the threshold of the pastor's message and will often be followed by an invitation to accept Jesus as one's Lord and Savior. Please don't hear judgmentalism in my description, as this tradition brought me to the Lord, taught me so much about the Holy Scriptures, gave to me a strong appreciation for weekly observance of the Lord's Supper, and a conviction to live a life of faith and to lead others to that faith in their lives.

The faith I received as a child, I first received in my Christian home. Dad and Mother were devout believers who were very active in their local church community. The Catholic Church refers to these churches as *ecclesial communities*, because they are not churches in the strictest and fullest sense that we understand. They do not honor the authority of Mother Church or the leadership of our Holy Father. Yet, these communities are devoted to the good news of the Gospel of Jesus Christ—*that there is salvation in no other name and that at His name every knee should bow and every tongue confess that He is Lord"* (Acts 4:12; Philippians 2:10-11). My parents made sure I was at church every Sunday, sitting in our "family pew," singing loudly, praying fervently, and listening attentively to the sermon. I'm not saying I was true to those requirements on a regular basis, and there were those occasions where I recall being taken out of the service to *have a word with my dad...* Needless to say, my return to the pew was followed by a strict adherence to what was going on, not to mention a little soreness as I sat on that wooden seat. I also remember my mother singing in the choir that was seated up front to the left of the pulpit, and she would keep a diligent eye on us. If my two brothers and I were misbehaving, she could throw a look our way with laser precision that sent the message quite clearly that we had better shape up, settle down, and straighten up!

Naturally, it was always my brothers' fault, and during the scolding in the car you could hear the *recessional chant* repeated again and again— *"He started it! I didn't do anything!"*

As Catholics, we are instructed to attend (at least) weekly Mass on Sunday or the anticipatory Mass on Saturday evening. But it doesn't end there. We are also to recognize the sanctity of our homes and families. That word *sanctity* comes from the same root from which we get several other words you're familiar with, including: *saint, sanctified and sanctification*. It is a transliteration (a new English word that sounds like the original word) from the Latin word *sanctus*, meaning "holy" or "sacred." The Latin comes to us from the Greek term *hagios* and behind the Greek is the Hebrew term found in the Old Testament—*kadosh*. In its literal sense, *kadosh* means "to be set apart for a special purpose." Most of these terms were not new to the Israelites (known as the Jews after the destruction of the Northern Kingdom of Israel). Rather the terms were drawn from the common usage in those days of long ago. This word would have been used to denote something in the home that was very special and should be *separated* from the common items in the house. Perhaps it was the fine utensils that were reserved only for special occasions, much like we might do with the Christmas dishes or the polished silver.

Do you recall our discussion of Isaiah's encounter with God in the Temple in Jerusalem? What was the chant he made as he beheld the glory of God? *Holy, Holy, Holy*. And don't forget that this trait is the only one used in the superlative of the Almighty. So if we want to really describe God in His essence, we would say He is Holy. This is the term that is used by the New Testament writers to describe the people of the Church of Jesus Christ. Hear the words of our first Pope, St. Peter: "...*like living stones, let yourselves be built into a spiritual house, to be a holy priesthood, to offer spiritual sacrifices acceptable to God through Jesus Christ*" (1 Peter 2:5). The Church extends this metaphor to the level of the truth that "*the family is, so to speak, the domestic church*" (Lumen Gentium #11). What does that mean? It means that our homes are to be set apart as holy places where we participate in godly service.

Furthermore, a father is called to serve in this home church as the priest, ministering to his wife and children, by virtue of his baptism. The primary task of the priest in the Old Testament and in our age of Christianity is to offer sacrifice to our God. Of course, in a general sense we are all called to make of ourselves a "*living sacrifice, holy and pleasing to God,*" which we are told is "*(our) spiritual worship*" (Romans 12:1). Fathers are to take the lead in this work of sacrifice to sanctify our marriages and families and even our homes as holy places wherein a form of spiritual worship takes place. That certainly raises the stakes on the requirements of a husband and father, doesn't it? A sad truth is that, despite our calling to serve as the priestly leaders of our domestic church households, it is too often found that we shirk our obligation to carry out that work, leaving it to our wives to carry the load in bringing spirituality into our homes.

We celebrated the feast of the Holy Family last Sunday, a commemoration of the family unit itself, looking to the family of our Lord as the supreme example of what it means to be family. Such an incredible consolation and hope comes to us in the realization that Jesus was born into and raised in a family. He knows the experience of living through the daily-ness of eating meals together, carrying out chores, talking through differences, dealing with personality quirks, celebrating birthdays, going to synagogue together and every other aspect of family life. Although we read little of the family unit of Jesus in the Gospel accounts, there is no reason to assume His world was all that unique from any of our own. My college classmate, Rich Mullins, expressed these thoughts in his song, *Boy Like Me/Man Like You*[11].

You was a baby like I was once

You was cryin' in the early mornin'

You was born in a stable Lord

Reid Memorial is where I was born

They wrapped you in swaddling clothes

Me they dressed in baby blue

Well, I was twelve years old in the meeting house

Listening to the old men pray

Well, I was tryin' hard to figure out

What it was that they was tryin' to say

There you were in the temple

They said, "You weren't old enough to know the things you knew"

Well did you grow up hungry?

Did you grow up fast?

Did the little girls giggle when you walked past?

Did you wonder what it was that made them laugh?

And did they tell you stories 'bout the saints of old

Stories about their faith

They say stories like that make a boy grow bold

Stories like that make a man walk straight

You was a boy like I was once

But was you a boy like me

Well, I grew up around Indiana

You grew up around Galilee

And if I ever really do grow up

Lord I want to grow up and be just like you

Did you wrestle with a dog and lick his nose?

Did you play beneath the spray

THE LITURGY OF MARRIAGE • 187

Of a water hose?

Did you ever make angels in the winter snow?

Did you ever get scared

Playing hide and seek?

Did you try not to cry

When you scraped your knee?

Did you ever skip a rock across a quiet creek?

And I really may just grow up

And be like you someday

Mullins took some criticism for portraying Jesus in such a human manner, but in his defense, he was only giving us a glimpse into the human nature of the Second Person of the Blessed Trinity. This is the glorious truth of the Incarnation: God entered the universe in the form of an infant, born into a human family to know the life we all live in some form or another. But this is not to be a theological truth held captive in the ivory towers of the faith, but rather a source of great inspiration for us as we follow in the example of this sacred family. We may not have the details of their lives, yet we can be assured they navigated the same kinds of challenges we face in this 21st century. I don't think Joseph delivered lengthy homilies to his son, but I do suspect he shared countless life lessons over the years, however many they had together. Some were likely in the wood shop as they completed one of his customer's jobs. Like my experience with my father, Jesus probably studied his earthly father to understand him, respect him, and learn from him.

It is too daunting for us husbands to consider assuming the role of the *domestic priest* if we have a view that requires stuffy ritualism and perfectionistic piety. The spiritual head of his home will offer his wife and children a quiet example of trustworthiness in the face of life's uncertainties. He brings a confidence in God's sovereign control that will secure his family amid any storm and, assuredly, the storms will come. It is not an extreme statement to say that family life can be chaotic at times and that during those times even the wisest of us will step back from that chaos and negotiate the alternatives. We will either follow the course of our first father, Adam, and retreat from the confusion, abandoning our families to chart their course without our priestly involvement, or we will follow the example of Joseph who must have felt utterly inept and incapable of carrying out any kind of priestly fatherhood with his son, the eternal High Priest of the ages. But he did fulfill that role, probably not perfectly with his sinless son, but still with a consistency that gave Jesus a taste of family security from the perspective of the flesh.

Kane sits in front of me with Megan—his wife of six years. They were referred for counseling by her family physician who saw the signs of both depression and despair in this woman whose womb was barren. In my experience the eyes tell the real story. Words may deceive, but the eyes always speak truth. Hers told a story of deep hurt and loneliness, not just for the infertile condition of her body, but the distance she felt from her husband. He was not insensitive to the pain, just bewildered at how to respond to it. And to make matters more difficult, he wrestled with his own pain and grief. His eyes told a slightly different story—one of guilt and inadequacy. My task is to nudge them toward each other to bridge the chasm of chaos the crisis brought to them. I said only five words to them, *"Turn, look at each other."* In that moment the emptiness was replaced with hopeful consolation and I was again privileged to have a front seat to behold God in his grace-filled sacrament of marriage.

Bringing It Home

The homily is that few minutes in the Mass when you get to hear the Priest share from his heart what the Scripture readings meant to him and what he thinks we most need to hear and understand from those inspired words of the Bible. Recently, at the encouragement of Matthew Kelly, I started taking a journal to Mass to make notes during the homily. I have to say it has definitely helped me to listen more carefully and allow the Spirit to teach, convict and console me. Try it and see if you experience the same results.

THE HOMILY AT HOME: THE DOMESTIC CHURCH

1. Do you find your mind drifting during the homily of the Mass? Starting the practice of a *Mass Journal* is one way to keep your mind more focused on what God is saying to you through the priest. Would you be willing to try this for a month? If not, what other ways could you make the teachings of the homily in Mass more personal and relevant? For example, making the Sunday brunch or lunch an opportunity to talk about how the message influenced you and what you gained from it?

2. Isaiah was, needless to say, surprised and even shocked by God in the Temple. If God were to appear to you—which He does every time you open the Bible, every time you celebrate the Mass, every time you participate in the Sacrament of Reconciliation—what would you be most surprised about? How has God surprised you so far in your life?

3. What are some lessons your father taught you about being a husband? Your mother taught you about being a wife? For some who do not have strong parent role models for marriage, consider other couples who have influenced your attitude about being a husband and wife and your overall philosophy of marriage.

TRY THIS EXERCISE

This exercise will definitely need to be one you plan and carry out together with husbands probably taking the lead from your wives. Locate a place in your home where you could create a kind of *family altar*—a place set apart and dedicated to prayer, meditation, Scripture reading, and even adoration of our Lord. Consider what pictures of our Lord, the Holy Family, or our Lady you might want to use for décor. Perhaps the words or prayer of a favorite saint would be framed. Have a place for your rosaries and maybe a candle or two. Consider having a priest come and bless the place, consecrating it as sacred space in your home. And what a wonderful place for reconciliation it could be, a place where the two of you would come when things have broken down between you. Imagine coming home after a spat that morning before you left for the day and now finding your spouse sitting in a chair at the family altar, praying and waiting for you to join. A place of reconciliation. Every marriage needs such a place. Create your own in your home!

THE HOLY FAMILY PRAYER

Jesus, Son of God and Son of Mary, bless our family.

Graciously inspire in us the unity, peace, and mutual love that you found in your own family in the little town of Nazareth.

Mary, Mother of Jesus and Our Mother, nourish our family with your faith and your love. Keep us close to your Son, Jesus, in all our sorrows and joys.

Joseph, Foster-father to Jesus, guardian and spouse of Mary, keep our family safe from harm. Help us in all times of discouragement or anxiety.

Holy Family of Nazareth, make our family one with you. Help us to be instruments of peace. Grant that love, strengthened by grace, may prove mightier than all the weaknesses and trials through which our families sometimes pass. May we always have God at the center of our hearts and homes until we are all one family, happy and at peace in our true home with you. Amen.

CHAPTER NINE

The Creed
Meaning What We Say

W e live in a day governed by the principle of tolerance. In this twenty-first century postmodern culture, it is considered by many to be almost immoral to question someone's beliefs. One belief is considered as good as another and contradiction is seen as just a misunderstanding. Such irrationality stands in contrast to the teachings of Scripture, wherein we read account after account of men and women of faith who sacrificed their very lives for their strongly held beliefs. Our beliefs define who we are, giving shape to our identities and purpose to our lives. Marriage is the most profoundly close relationship we will ever have with another person. It necessitates that our beliefs be as compatible as possible. Not that we have to agree on everything, but there should not be any glaring core beliefs that are in conflict between two people considering the sacrament of marriage.

Having a sacred liturgy for marriage means those beliefs will not end once we exit the doors of the parish after Mass. Holding to the essential elements of Christianity should motivate us to live differently in our homes and relate with a Christ-like love toward our loved ones. That is no small feat when we consider the daily challenges we all face when our personalities clash. We stand up during the celebration of the Mass and recite those familiar words, which have been committed to memory over the years.

I believe in one God, the Father Almighty, maker of heaven and earth, of all things visible and invisible. I believe in one Lord Jesus Christ, the Only Begotten Son of God, born of the Father before all ages. God from God, Light from Light, true God from true God, begotten, not made, consubstantial with the Father; through him all things were made. For us men and for our salvation he came down from heaven, and by the Holy Spirit was incarnate of the Virgin Mary, and became man.

For our sake he was crucified under Pontius Pilate, he suffered death and was buried, and rose again on the third day in accordance with the Scriptures.

He ascended into heaven and is seated at the right hand of the Father. He will come again in glory to judge the living and the dead and his kingdom will have no end.

I believe in the Holy Spirit, the Lord, the giver of life, who proceeds from the Father and the Son, who with the Father and the Son is adored and glorified, who has spoken through the prophets.

I believe in one, holy, catholic and apostolic Church. I confess one baptism for the forgiveness of sins and I look forward to the resurrection of the dead and the life of the world to come. Amen.[12]

The term is anglicized from the Latin word *credo*, meaning "I believe." In my Protestant days, the term "creed" implied something artificially contrived by men in their efforts to reduce the Scriptures to a set of statements reflecting only a limited and partial truth. Now I have come to realize that we all have our creeds and creedal statements, regardless of ecclesiastical affiliations.

We believe there is one God, not many gods—a belief that brings sovereignty into the world and into our marriages. He is Father, bringing life into all relationships. He chose to enter this world through marriage and family. This gives us great confidence that the God of the universe upholds the very institution itself. Believing that He lived as a man, experienced the temptations of life in a fallen world, yet remained without sin, we find hope that we too can rise above the temptations of our lives, especially those that will threaten the fabric of marriage. Believing in the eternal nature of our lives brings comfort in the face of the death of our loved ones. Believing in the life-giving reality of the Holy Spirit gives us the energy to press on with tenacious determination, trusting that His grace is sufficient. And believing in the true spirit of the catholicity of the Holy Catholic Church inspires us to know that we are not alone in the world. The Creator has endowed Mother Church with the inspired and living resources we need to respond faithfully throughout the course of marriage.

But does it really matter if a husband and wife share common beliefs in religion? Well, at the outset it might not be that important since neither one may be practicing their faith all that much. Studies do support this observation, finding that religion only is a problem when both partners are more consistently trying to live out their faith beliefs. Of course, that doesn't mean two atheists will get along fine in marriage, because we all know that not having a belief system *is* its own belief system. In the family life cycle, where religious practice will predictably increase is at the event of parenthood. The first child comes on the marital scene and this prompts the parents to begin asking themselves some philosophical questions about life, the future, security, eternity, and the effect of such contemplation will often lead one back to his or her faith roots. One tends to wonder, *after all, what did my parents teach me about such matters? If it was good enough for them, then it's good enough for me and my children.*

As a convert to the Catholic Church, I tend to place more emphasis on the need to study in preparation for making a choice about religious affiliation. It seems too many people opt for one church over another for rather un-theological reasons. For one person, it might be the beauty of the building, while for another the style of music. Others are drawn to the quality of the preaching. Still others want to make certain the childcare is responsible and trustworthy. And, of course, there are those who just want to make sure they serve good coffee and donuts after the service.

From my vantage point, I would like to see people asking some deeper questions in their search for religion and faith. Questions like: *Is there a god? How do I know? Has he spoken? Can I trust the Bible? Where did the Bible come from? Did Jesus establish a Church? If so, which one? What is the history of the Church? Why do we have so many different churches? Do all Christian churches believe the same thing? What are the differences and why?* Such questions will drive a process of study from which will emerge a strong set of beliefs and maybe just lead you to the beliefs stated in the Nicene Creed (the profession of the Christian faith approved at the Council of Constantinople in 381) itself. Selah!

Let me recommend a good exercise for you and your spouse. Think through some questions about your own beliefs. Here are a few to help you get started with the process:

Do you believe in God? Why?

Where were your beliefs about God formed and developed?

Have you ever tried to substantiate your beliefs about God? How?

What doubts do you struggle with about God?

How have you resolved those doubts and questions?

What do you believe about religion?

Why did you choose to practice the religious faith that you do?

These are deep philosophical and theological questions that can lead to some great discussions for the two of you and the typical outcome of such dialogue is a strengthening of your marital faith. Essentially, that is the purpose of this book, to solidify your Christian faith as an integral part of the fabric of your marriage. As you wrestle with these questions, don't stop at the point of confusion. Rather, push through it to do some research to find the answers. Most of them are out there, as you're not the first to pose the question. One of the beautiful aspects of our Catholic tradition is the historical development of theology over the two millennia since Christ established His Church. You can start with a Bible in one hand and the Catechism of the Catholic Church in the other hand. That will probably carry you 75% of the way through the confusion and then you can turn to your parish priest to either find the answers, direction or resources to go the rest of the way. Now, in the final analysis, you'll likely be left with a certain amount of doubt and confusion. Don't be surprised or disheartened by this. Keep the goal at certitude, not certainty and remember the words of Blessed John Henry Newman, *"Ten thousand difficulties do not make a doubt."* He also took that proverbial *swim* across the Tiber.

When I was studying Catholicism prior to my conversion, I tried to exhaust as many sources of information as I could, reading books and articles, having challenging discussions and even debates, and listening to classes and homilies incessantly.

At one point, I came to the realization I just shared with you—be content with certitude. Generally speaking, the difference between certitude and certainty is that degree of unknowingness where our questions cannot be answered, or at least not at this time. My own conclusion was and still is that I had more answers than not and knowing what I had come to discover through my research gave me the confidence that there were more answers and explanations out there for the unanswered questions, which would resolve the remaining confusion if I had that information.

Be cautious about aligning yourself with anyone who tells you they have all the answers to the eternal questions of life. As well, use discretion with those who do the same thing with marriage. My field of study and practice has a rich empirical history that should elicit a trust in what we can offer our clients by way of assistance, guidance, and resources for improvement and resolution. Nevertheless, exercise discernment when someone comes across a little too "expert-ish." I like to tell the couples who come to me for therapy that counseling is a collaborative effort in which we work together to find the best course through their difficulties. You've already heard me say that I'm not an expert on marriage, just a student of marriage. I love the prospect of meeting each new couple who walks through the doors of my office and am anxious to hear their story, enter that story and hopefully involve myself with them in a manner that ultimately restores some of the joy and hope in that story.

One more comment on this topic of beliefs. If you find yourself in need of some counseling support for your relationship, be sure to do your homework before entering treatment with someone to help you work on your marriage. Remember that every provider has his or her own belief system and that worldview may influence the direction you go in your counseling. Now, the ethical codes of conduct to which we must subscribe and observe are designed to protect the client(s) from such undue influence, but that influence can still be felt in the therapeutic experience. So, unlike the physician whose prescriptions for antibiotics and vaccinations will have an effect regardless of how you feel about that healthcare provider, the counselor and your relationship with that counselor can and usually will be a considerable factor in your marriage counseling experience.

Bringing It Home

Did you find yourself thinking about your own personal beliefs as you read through this chapter? Whether about God, the Church, eternity, marriage, work, or any other topic, we probably all need to come to some position that we can affirm with certainty that this is our belief. The process of determining and then verifying our beliefs is not an easy one and it will and should require considerable time and effort. So let this be an opportunity for you to step back and review your own worldview, taking seriously your stand on the important matters of life.

THE CREED

1. You recite the Nicene Creed each week during the Mass as the prelude to the liturgy of the Eucharist. What elements of the Creed give you pause and cause you to wonder? Recite the Creed slowly and listen carefully as the words leave your lips. Enter the awe of the truths to which you give voice.

2. What aspects of our Catholic faith have been a source of tension and even conflict for the two of you in your

marriage? If there are none, say a prayer of thanksgiving and then recite the Nicene Creed together out loud as a prayer.

3. If you could ask God one question about our faith what would it be? Talk about it as a couple and consider taking it together to your priest to see what he might have to say about it.

TRY THIS EXERCISE

In this exercise, I'd like the two of you to think about your beliefs, positions, and opinions on a variety of subjects. Try to put any sense of needing to be right or have all the answers aside and just enter into an open and accepting dialogue, curious about your partner's ideas. Take some current issue topics and then ask yourselves a few questions about each one, like—*What do you think is the right thing to do? Why? Does our Catholic faith say anything about this subject? Looking at the Catechism of the Catholic Church, can we find a principle or teaching that is relevant?*

EXAMPLES:

- Contraception
- Infertility

- Obligation to attend the Mass
- Adherence to the Church's teachings
- Your calling as a married couple

PART THREE

The Liturgy of the Eucharist

CHAPTER TEN

The Lord's Prayer
Prayer Makes a Difference

In 2003 I entered the Roman Catholic Church, coming to a culmination of three years of arduous study only to open the door to another three years of arduous study to complete some unfinished business. My divorce in 1989 forced me to put my doctoral studies on hold indefinitely, but not my dream. Originally, I had planned to complete my PhD by the age of 35. Life did not work out according to my plan and the truth is, I'm not sure it ever does. Those of us in the field of healthcare must take at least one course in research, but the Master of Arts or Master of Science degree is not a research degree and research was what intrigued me, especially in faith-based treatments and their effectiveness. I wanted to better understand research, not just how to better interpret the existing studies in my field—I wanted to become more of a practitioner-researcher. There is a great need for professionals in the field of marriage and family therapy to conduct more clinic-based research. You see, much of the research is done at the university level and setting, which is not a bad thing, but not always true to life. There are limits as to how much we can generalize findings that are done at a university among college or graduate age married students to the population at large.

So, in 2003 I resumed my studies toward a terminal degree in a program at a university that would allow me to maintain my clinical work as a therapist and yet, through residency work, still complete the PhD program. In 2005 I began work on my dissertation, brainstorming the kind of research I wanted to do as my first effort. My background in the ministry and my strong Christian faith led me to think seriously about doing some work to compare purely secular treatments against faith-based treatments for a psychological condition. Where I landed was in the context of marriage and marital therapy. I wrestled with a wide variety of ideas and questions. Can a couple improve their marriage if they go to Mass every day for a month? What about going to Confession once a week for six months? Or maybe reading a chapter of the Bible every day for a month might move a couple's marriage up the scale of improvement. It can be a fascinating process to throw out questions like these and come up with a vast number of ideas for further study.

Then I started thinking about the idea of prayer. Would praying make a difference in a couple's relationship? After all, we often say that prayer is effective. St. James even said, *"The fervent prayer of a righteous person is very powerful"* (James

5:16). We believe in the power of prayer, but would that belief be supported by empirical research into its effectiveness? That was my challenge and I was excited to take it on. The first order of business was to form the research question. Essentially it could be stated as *does prayer improve marital satisfaction?* It would, of course, be revised over the course of the year, but I at least had a starting place.

The next order of business was to investigate what had been done in this area previous to my planned study. It's been said that *a PhD knows a lot about a little.* I came to realize the truth in that statement as I started to explore the world of prayer. How surprising, yet reassuring, it was to discover the enormity of research that had already been conducted on the efficacy of prayer. Let me share just some of the highlights of my investigation.

Praying brings peace

Praying regularly has been shown to bring peace to many people, helping them to find better ways to cope with the painful parts of their lives, according to Harold Koenig, prominent and well respected researcher with the Center for Spirituality, Theology and Health at Duke University[13]. This is why most hospitals, even the non-religiously oriented ones, have a pastoral department or a chaplain among its personnel to provide care and spiritual support to patients and their families during a time of crisis and suffering. Prayer has the potential to improve a patient's attitude despite the medical crisis he may be going through, by changing the perception of the illness. Psychology tells us it is not the event or situation that determines our reaction, but our interpretation of the event. Someone may go through a season of suffering, but perspective will make all the difference in the world—whether one responds with denial, anger, sadness or acceptance. Of course, in the process of grieving our responses will change, but only as our attitudes and perceptions shift with the passage of time and the gaining of new mindsets.

There is yet another point to be made about praying together as a couple, and that is the benefit that comes from hearing your spouse speak words of affirmation, appreciation and supplication on your behalf. This is especially true if those words are specifically relevant to each other's personal needs that have been expressed or at least made evident recently. Imagine during the stress you find yourself under at work you hear your wife pray—" *Father, this is such a difficult time for Lance and I know how hard he's working. Please give him the strength to be diligent, but also the hope of relief. Amen.*" What if you were suffering from a chronic illness and you heard your husband pray— "*Lord, I don't like that Erin hurts so much of the time and pray you'll show me how I can encourage her more. Please give wisdom to her physician to find better ways or medicines for her illness and the pain it causes her. Amen.*"

Setting up my research

Let's get back to my research on prayer and how I decided to set up the experiment. The first step was to come up with a workable design for the study. I chose to conduct an experiment with 100 couples and see what would happen if I split them into two groups, had half of them praying together and the other half participating over the same time period in another proven effective exercise by Dr. John Gottman[14], which helps couples increase marital satisfaction. Most researchers who conduct studies on human behavior have to work very hard to control for those variables that can confound the process and weaken the results of the entire work. This was no less true in my case, which is why I limited the experiment to just thirty days. Any longer would have opened the door to too many of those factors affecting the participants and would have decreased my chances of determining whether the prayers would really be effective. At the same time, I was afraid that any shorter would not have been enough time to really make any notable difference.

With the methodology now in place and having gained approval from the Institutional Review Board (IRB) of the university, it was time to move ahead with trying to solicit at least eighty couples to participate in the experiment. My approach was to contact several Catholic and Protestant churches in our community and invite any married couples to join in the process. Somewhat to my surprise, we hit the eighty mark within just a few weeks, including six additional couples in case any of them might drop out during the study. We were ready to get started. An easy way to think about experiments like this would be to use the analogy of a study to determine the effectiveness of, say, a weight loss program. Obviously the first thing you'd do is weigh all those involved in the program before you get started and again after the completion of your program in order to see whether it worked and how well it worked. That's exactly what I did, however my focus was on their satisfaction as a couple, not weight.

I needed some way to measure the current level of satisfaction in their marriages. So I found a test that would do just that. Then I randomly divided them into the two groups, gave them their instructions and we were off to a 30-day experiment to see whether prayer would make a notable difference in improving marital satisfaction. At the conclusion of the period the couples were all re-tested to determine change and how much change. We also wanted to compare the two groups to see who did better. What is nice about this kind of research is that you end up with an enormous amount of data that you can then study in a wide number of ways. I wanted not only to compare the two groups against each other, I also was curious whether the Catholics or Protestants would do better.

We'll look at the findings, but first let's go over some of the demographics of the group. We had forty-six Catholic couples representing 54% of the total group and forty Protestant couples representing the other 46%. The couples represented a wide range of occupations, household incomes, ages, and years married. This enabled us to apply the results to a broader spectrum of the general population. At the outset of the study the testing revealed that the Catholic couples were in a more satisfied range on the average than the Protestant couples.

The Results

You spend months planning and preparing for a major project like this and months carrying it out. When collecting the data at the close of the thirty days by testing the couples again for their levels of satisfaction, you just hope and pray to see some results that will support the original hypothesis that prayer will make a positive difference in the satisfaction level of married couples. We plugged the numbers into the statistical formulas and the results supported what we as believers have known all along. Prayer really does work!

We could determine with confidence that the couples that spent their thirty days in prayer experienced a rise in their level of satisfaction. Some might want to attribute the gain to the marriage counseling some of the couples were involved in, but this didn't hold up either. In running these kind of analyses, we can control for certain known variables, which we did in the case of those who were receiving any marital treatment, and we found that the elevation of marital satisfaction remained constant for the praying couples over the thirty-day period.

We discovered one other interesting fact from our study worth mentioning. You may recall me saying that we had both Catholic and Protestant couples represented in the praying experiment. What was curious to me was that it was the Catholic group who experienced the greatest benefit. The Protestants also benefited from the exercise, just not to the degree that the Catholics did. Research is a wonderful way to lend support for our faith and, in this case, our faith-based interventions to help married couples, but we still must interpret the findings to really make sense of the results. This weighed heavily on my mind as I reviewed the outcome data and I finally reached a conclusion that the activity of praying specific prayers for one's spouse is more unusual for a Catholic couple than for Protestants. Attend a Protestant worship service and you will hear prayers that are much more conversational and personal than the formal prayers of the Catholic tradition. This is in no way meant to be a judgment against either form of prayer, just an observation that may suggest that Catholics experience something new and perhaps more helpful through the novelty of such personalized prayers.

I came full circle

In my ministry as an ordained Protestant pastor I frequently met with people in various life circumstances of illness, grief and distress, including married partners in times of despair and crisis. With about eight hours of undergraduate coursework in pastoral counseling and maybe an additional graduate course in the same. I was in no way prepared or qualified to address these kinds of problems. So, I did the only thing I knew to do and that was to share some passages from the Bible, listen and pray. Not infrequently I would imagine to myself how much more effective my work could be if I were just trained as a physician, a nurse or perhaps even a psychologist. After all, I naively thought, what good is it to read, listen and pray for someone going through the kind of pain these people were in?

Two earned degrees later in the fields of counseling and human services, I can now admit to having come full circle. Don't misunderstand me. My education in psychology has enabled me to gain incredible insight into the inner world of my clients and I am forever grateful for the influence of my professors, mentors and clinical supervisors. Yet, having said all that, I can truly admit that the most powerful and effective interventions I utilize in my work are to share the truth of God's Word, to listen compassionately, and to pray fervently for my clients. That word *compassion* comes to us from two Greek words that mean *with pain*. Isn't that the essential nature of healing—to enter the pain of others to be with them amid the pain? St. Paul had something to say about this concept of communal sharing during hurt in his words to the Corinthians,

"If one part suffers, all the parts suffer with it..." (1 Corinthians 12:26).

Recently I have been reading through the book of Job. Not too many people have experienced the kind of suffering this man of ancient times went through, but almost as bad as his pain was the poor counsel of his would-be friends who battered him with their harsh interpretations of his suffering in their supposed attempt to console him. They would have done better to have just sat with him and said nothing. The ancient Jews had a custom like this when someone in the community was grieving the death of a loved one. They would come and just sit with the person for seven days, known as *shiva* from the Hebrew word for seven. It's a beautiful ceremony of being present and listening as one passes through the shadow of grief. We could all probably gain much from our Jewish kindreds' practice.

What kind of prayers work?

Selecting the prayers for my research study was not easy. I considered writing my own prayers, but that's a little like writing your own test and it usually reduces the quality of the work. After some survey of the land, I settled on some beautiful and practical prayers from a couple of books written by Stormie Omartian[15]. She has dedicated her writing to the topic of prayer and includes numerous sample prayers in her books. Her prayers were well written, relevant to marital issues and even bound in small, affordable booklets that made it very easy for the couples to keep at their bedside for use each morning and night. If you have interest in the books you can find her website in the bibliography.

Catholics have a plethora of prayers available. Even the sign of the cross is a prayer, acknowledging the Trinity and reminding us that the Father, Son and Holy Spirit are with us always. The Our Father is a prayer that can recalibrate us to the need for reliance upon God for our daily needs to be met, as well as the need we all have for forgiveness and for the encouragement to give forgiveness to others. The Holy Rosary reorients us to the life of Christ and brings us into the awareness of how Jesus' life intersects with our own. Finally, the prayers of the saints over the centuries offer venues to commune with our Lord and deepen our faith while also nurturing our marriage relationship.

I encourage you to pray as a couple, whether you pray the prayers of the saints, the prayers of the ages, the prayers of others who have shared some of your experiences. The most important thing is that the two of you make time and room to pray. You will have to push against the natural inner resistances to share your soul and expose your needs. But you will find the results to be well worth it. Spiritual intimacy is not common and not easy. But it is the avenue to total oneness in your marriage. Don't wait. Begin today. Take your spouse's hand. Take a deep breath. And say the words. *"Can we pray?"*

Then do it and remember your own words will probably be the most powerful of all.

Bringing It Home

Did any of the findings about prayer noted in this chapter come as a surprise to you? Discovering the power of prayer can be a little shocking to some as we live in such a scientific world in which most things make sense from a rational point of view. Prayer doesn't usually fit into those neat categories of explanation and that can be a bit unsettling for us. At the same time, prayer can be exciting and can engender a hope on our part that there is more taking place in the world than what meets the eye.

THE LORD'S PRAYER
PRAYER MAKES A DIFFERENCE

---

1. When you examine your own prayer life what do you see? How would you evaluate your practice of prayer? Do you pray together as a couple? If not, what seems to get in the way? What difference do you think it would make if you started praying together regularly?

2. If a miracle is defined as God intervening in the material world, have you ever witnessed a miracle? Share it with your spouse.

3. If you had been approached to participate in my research study which group would you have chosen, the prayer group or the conventional marital therapy group? Why?

TRY THIS EXERCISE

Prayer is a private and personal experience, so this may prove a little embarrassing and challenging for you. But that's also the point of most of these exercises—to push you outside your comfort zones. In this one you are to write out a prayer for your marriage. It should be a prayer that speaks to the unique nature of *your* relationship and the particular issues, needs, and purpose or even mission, as you see it, of your marriage. Spend some time getting it right, working on finding the exact wording, almost like writing the lyrics to a song. Then after you both agree on the finished product, type it out and frame it. Put it on the altar you made earlier and recite it regularly, if not daily, as your special marital prayer to the Lord.

CHAPTER ELEVEN

A Sign of Peace
The 12 Most Difficult Words to Say

W e hear the words at every Mass: *"Lord, have mercy."* These beautiful words remind us who we are— sinners in need of His grace. Humility is a cure for most marriages, as it counters the pride that keeps us from the pursuit of peaceful reconciliation. Jesus was asked on one occasion why the ancient deliverer Moses gave to the Israelites the option to divorce their spouses. His response was a simple and straightforward one: He said it was because of the hardness of their hearts. The therapist in me identifies that hardness as resistance, something we encounter in our work every day. It is the part of the client who says, "No way will I change!" when the person is asking for help to do just that—change. We all have that part and it can grow under certain conditions to the point where we find ourselves hardened.

We also know very well what happens after we offer the prayer of our Lord in the Mass and are directed to *share the peace* with those around us. What do these strange words mean, but to extend an invitation to be in a reconciled place with our brothers and sisters. To be reconciled is to be at peace. The absence of peace is broken relationship.

Many a marriage has been destroyed by this toxic condition. Against the hardened heart therapy is rendered ineffective. Did you know our Lord gave us the actual cause of divorce? Ask any number of people why and when divorce would be considered acceptable and they'll usually defend the termination of a marriage based on one or a combination of the three "A's", *Adultery*, *Addiction* or *Abuse*. Now please don't misunderstand me on this. All these are tragic and must not be tolerated in a marriage. However, having said that I would add that they do not cause the divorce. Let's look at Jesus' answer carefully as found in Matthew's account.

> Some Pharisees approached him, and tested him, saying, "Is it lawful for a man to divorce his wife for any cause whatever?" He said in reply, "Have you not read that from the beginning the Creator 'made them male and female' and said, 'For this reason a man shall leave his father and mother and be joined to his wife, and the two shall become one flesh'? So they are no longer two, but one flesh. Therefore, what God has joined together, no human being must separate." They said to him, "Then why did Moses command that the man give the woman a bill of divorce and dismiss

[her]?" He said to them, "Because of the hardness of your hearts Moses allowed you to divorce your wives, but from the beginning it was not so. I say to you, whoever divorces his wife (unless the marriage is unlawful) and marries another commits adultery." (Matthew 19:3-9)

There are several crucial points to be made from this passage in the Gospels about marriage. First, perpetual oneness as the proper condition of the sacrament of marriage is made abundantly clear by our Lord. Second, human endeavors to separate the relationship do not supersede the divine covenant the two have entered. Third, the reason, then, for divorce comes down to a heart condition—*hardness of the heart*. Call it stubbornness, rebellion, or false pride, but it is a resistance to reconciliation that results in the demise of a marriage. Fourth, Jesus acknowledges the possibility of a marriage that is *"unlawful,"* which means that it did not meet the standards of covenant or sacrament. This is ordinarily determined today through the annulment process of the Church when the marital tribunal of a diocese reviews the testimony of a couple and makes the decision as to the nullity of the marriage from the moment of consent. Finally, it is evident in the teaching of Jesus that adultery is not the cause of divorce, but rather the result of divorce when the marriage is considered valid in God's eyes.

I work with couples all too frequently in my practice whose marriages have been ravaged by adultery, addiction and abuse (though usually at the emotional level rather than physical). In most those cases, the couples find their way back to a place of reconciliation. When they don't, it is because the damage wreaked on the relationship has left one or both partners hardened beyond repair. The heart is that inner sanctum of the person with a lock that must be opened from within. The best efforts of a spouse seeking forgiveness will fall on deaf ears when the offended partner is not able to soften his or her heart. It saddens me when I observe that scene of passionate pleading from the one and obstinate resistance from the other. In the end *"No"* always wins out.

The Marital Sentiment

This would be a good place to talk about one of the most predictable aspects of the marriage relationship. We usually call it the *marital sentiment*. The construct has to do with the partners' ways of viewing each other in the relationship. It was first identified by Dr. Robert Weiss, prominent researcher on marriage, as he was studying spousal reactions during marital interaction[16]. He noted that it is based on a subjective interpretation by the marriage partner, rather than objective data from the actual interaction of the two people, and can lead to a cognitive evaluation that frequently skews the perception of the spouse negatively.

The sentiment incorporates both attitude and motivation; how the person sees the spouse and how willing he or she is to work on the issues troubling the couple. Assisting a person in altering his perception of the marriage partner, particularly when the relationship has deteriorated into a significant condition of distress, is a formidable task for anyone, be it counselor, priest, friend or family member.

This can all be a little confusing, so let me illustrate what it is we're talking about. Take a couple who have been dating for some six months and just watch them. Notice how he treats her in such a caring and loving way, always tending to her needs and wishes. Observe her as she studies his every move, paying close attention to those characteristic mannerisms she has come to love about him. We would naturally assess the marital sentiment of these two lovebirds as extremely positive. In fact, that sentiment is so highly skewed in the positive direction that it will spill over and even override much of the negativity that may occur in the couple's interaction. For example, say he tells her he'll meet her and their friends at the restaurant by six, but it turns out he forgot he had to stop off at the post office to mail a package to his mother. Meanwhile, she's back having drinks and appetizers with the friends waiting for his arrival, but instead of badmouthing him about his chronic lateness, she is making excuses for him and reminding their friends just how busy her partner is with all the many demands of his life. At 6:25 he finally arrives and she greets him with a kiss. All is well in Camelot! That, my friends, is what we call *Positive Sentiment Override*. They have built up such a surplus of positivity in their relationship that he could afford to *borrow* some against his negative behavior on this occasion.

Now clearly it must be pointed out that the proverbial emotional tank of their relationship sentiment is not static and can be used up if the two are not careful to attend to it through regular positive behavior. So let's now fast forward the calendar on this same couple seven years later and observe another scene not all that dissimilar to the first. But this time they've been married for six years, have two preschoolers, a hefty mortgage, a couple maxed out credit cards, and are both exhausted. Once again he is running late while she is waiting at the restaurant with their friends. Something's very different this time as she now cannot stop complaining to their friends about how tired she is of being last on his list of priorities. She rants and raves at how irresponsible and uncaring he is toward her and adds that she's just about at the end of her rope. Then enters *Prince Charming* with a smile on his face and a surprise single red rose in his hand to give his bride of six years. As he leans over to greet her with a kiss she turns her head and pulls away as his lips graze her cheek. Their friends look down at their drinks and try not to notice the awkward scene. And that, sadly, is what we call *Negative Sentiment Override*. The emotional bank account is depleted and now even his positive efforts are met with rejection.

This negativity leads to a negative feedback loop in which the individual falls into what we refer to as a *confirmation bias*, believing the worst about the partner and looking for anything that will confirm the negative belief. But it gets worse. The negative perception leads to a negative interpretation of the behavior of the partner, as if to say, "he's doing this on purpose!" Reality is lost on the altar of misperception. Gracious benefits of the doubt are replaced now with contempt, filtering out even the sincerest efforts to repair the ruins of the relationship.

And just when you think it can't get any worse, it does. The negativity reaches a level where the more distressed partner seems to do a re-write of their marital history. Don't misunderstand me. I'm not saying he or she is making up lies. It's worse than that in a way. She doesn't realize it, but her mind is filtering out so much of the good of their relational story that she is left now with just the dregs of negativity, able only to remember the bad times that feed her now depleted and negative sentiment. Listening to this complainant drone on and on about how badly the spouse has treated her, leaves you unable to do anything other than lend your full support for leaving the awful person at the soonest possible date. After all, who would be expected to stay married to someone who has such a history?

One partner wants out desperately, but feels stuck. The other is just as desperate to save the marriage, but feels helpless. Welcome to my world and the condition of 90% of the couples who seek marriage counseling. It is a sad movie to watch and I see it repeated countless times. The death of a marriage that was intended by both partners to take them through all the joys, mountaintops, twists and turns of life is disturbing. Witnessing this process brings me to grieve but it also motivates me to try with all my skill and experience to turn back the tide of toxic negativity.

One of the methods I use to do that is to take a history of their relationship. As I mentioned, that history may be tainted with negativity and represent a skewed accounting, but if I probe delicately and curiously, I might be able to stir up some good memories and even the feelings that accompany those stories. *"How did the two of you meet?"* is followed by a story of that first encounter. *"What was your first impression of him?"* I ask as I search desperately for a hint of that early attraction. I trace through the story of their lives looking for and watering with my words the seeds of hope. If I can find those seeds I have something to work with, to shape and mold back together. It is a dance that exhausts me and exhilarates me all at the same time. St. Paul exhorts us to be *ambassadors of reconciliation* (2 Corinthians 5:20)—a calling I take seriously in my work. Among the effects of this fallen world, brokenness is perhaps nowhere more evident than in a failing marriage.

What does all this have to do with the sign of peace during the Mass? Jesus had some strong words for us around worship that seem to have application here. In the famous sermon on the mount He admonishes:

Therefore, if you bring your gift to the altar, and there recall that your brother has anything against you, leave your gift there at the altar, go first and be reconciled with your brother, and then come and offer your gift.. (Matthew 5:23-24).

His words echo the words of the prophets centuries before when they called back the children of Israel from their spiritual idolatry, which was tantamount to the sin of spiritual adultery against their Holy Husband. The great prophet of Israel, Isaiah implores the people of his time:

"What do I care for the multitude of your sacrifices? Says the LORD... When you come to appear before me, who asks these things of you? Trample my courts no more! To bring offerings is useless; incense is an abomination to me... Your new moons and festivals I detest; they weigh me down, I tire of the load. When you spread out your hands, I will close my eyes to you; Though you pray the more, I will not listen." (Isaiah 11:11-15)

These words reveal the kind of message that makes so many people avoid the reading of the Old Testament, yet if we read on we will see why God is so angry that He would reject the very offerings he once required of His bride. "...learn to do good. Make justice your aim: redress the wronged, hear the orphan's plea, defend the widow." (Isaiah 1:17) We dare not stop until we hear the sweet message of redemption available to us from the Lord. "Come now, let us set things right, says the LORD: Though your sins be like scarlet, they may become white as snow; Though they be red like crimson, they may become white as wool." (Isaiah 1:18)

If Almighty God could bring the hope of reconciliation to his bride Israel, who are we to think His hand is too short to restore the joy of marital love to a couple in severe distress? But before that restoration can take place, there must be a conviction of the soul that fosters a letting go of resentment so the work of healing can occur. The humility required of the partners for this miracle to happen does not come without a cost. That cost comes in the form of exposure to further pain in the relationship—a pain that prompted the self-protective withdrawal from the marriage. And now I am suggesting, even recommending, you step back into the fire and allow God to perform his miracle of marital redemption.

I write these words knowing full well that I will now lose some of you who are angry, filled with resentment and whose minds are already made up with the resolution to leave your marriage because of the untold pain you have endured all these years. And yet, unless that pain has come in the form of one or a combination of what we call the three A's—Abuse, Adultery and/or Active Addiction, I encourage you to find God's protection and grace to be sufficient to return to the love of your youth (Malachi 2:15).

A familiar passage from the Old Testament about divorce is Malachi 2:16, where the prophet by the same name (which means in the Hebrew—*my messenger*) boldly tells the ancient Jews, *"Did he not make them one, with flesh and spirit? And what does the One require? Godly offspring! You should be on guard, then, for your life, and do not break faith with the wife of your youth. For I hate divorce, says the LORD, the God of Israel, And the one who covers his garment with violence, says the LORD of hosts. You should be on guard, then, for your life, and you must not break faith.* (Malachi 2:14-16).

Now let me make a few observations based on this strong passage against divorce. First, we should note that God is citing the basis for faithfulness as the oneness He has called all of us into as part of His family. This is the oneness we demonstrate just before the Eucharist when we recite the prayer Jesus taught us and then do just what he prayed we would do— *"...forgive us our trespasses as we forgive those who trespass against us..."* Participation in the Holy Eucharist necessitates a spirit of unity in our lives. St. Paul told the Corinthians, *"When you meet in one place, then, it is not to eat the Lord's supper, for in eating, each one goes ahead with his own supper, and one goes hungry while another gets drunk...Therefore whoever eats the bread or drinks the cup of the Lord unworthily will have to answer for the body and blood of the Lord."* (I Corinthians 11: 20-27). He concludes powerfully, *"A person should examine himself, and so eat the bread and drink the cup. For anyone who eats and drinks without discerning the body, eats and drinks judgment on himself"* (vv.28-29). The principle seems clear that if oneness in our relationships is compromised, let alone severed, we have an obligation to do all possible to restore oneness and unity as part of our worship and especially before we partake of the body and blood of Jesus Christ.

Not only do we see the rationale of relationship for oneness, but note the emphatic focus on children. We see that this restoration of relationship is so critical to God that He rejects the offerings we bring before Him if there is a spirit and lifestyle of hard-heartedness among us. He desires us to enter a spirit of humility where we are open to receive His mercy that can wash away the blemish of bitter resentment. No one is saying this will be easy, but the Psalmist consistently reminds us to be of a contrite spirit. King David discovered this reality after his own departure of his marriage into adultery, and in humble repentance wrote—*"For you do not desire sacrifice or I would give it; a burnt offering you would not accept. My sacrifice, O God, is a contrite spirit; a contrite, humbled heart, O God, you will not scorn* (Psalm 51: 18-19). This may anger some of you reading these words. Go beneath your anger to see the hurt and fear that has driven you to leave your spouse, whether emotionally, physically or even legally.

And one final point from the passage in Malachi—not only do we see the rationale of relationship for oneness, the emphatic focus is on the children. The prophet writes, *"And what does the One require? Godly offspring"* (v.15). Long before the researchers discovered the multiple and deleterious effects of divorce on children, the Lord gave these words to His people. Haven't we witnessed how a broken family affects the life course of the children of the marriage? Not that they become mentally ill or even lose their faith altogether, but they are left to face life without the model and refuge of marital fidelity from their parents.

So, we are called to be a people of *peace*. This is not a calling to a superficial experience of good feelings that ignores the seriousness of conflicting values, unresolvable tensions and irretrievable brokenness, but a calling to be a people who will do everything within our power and, even more, the power of God to restore and reconcile with those who have done us wrong and those whom we have done wrong. Only then are we ready to kneel before the Holy Eucharist in humble and contrite thanksgiving.

The twelve most difficult words to say, but also the twelve most powerful words to speak!

Use them often...

"I was wrong

I am sorry

please forgive me

I love you!"

Bringing It Home

"Lord, have mercy!" Such sincere and beautiful words of desire we offer to God. The hardening of our hearts is a temptation that any of us can face in our lives and it can turn us away from the humble walk wherein we seek out the Lord's mercy. A marriage intoxicated with the sin of pride will likely find itself embroiled in bitter conflict with spouses unwilling to enter a spirit of repentance where a spirit of peaceful reconciliation can re-emerge. May our hearts ever be open to the Spirit's call to humility.

A SIGN OF PEACE
THE 12 MOST DIFFICULT WORDS TO SAY

---

1. What do you think about Jesus' assessment on divorce in Matthew 19:3-9? Is the hardness of heart, or pride, really the core problem in a marriage that is failing or has failed? Have you witnessed this in others' marriages that have failed? Have you experienced this hardness in your own relationship?

2. How is your *marital sentiment* toward your spouse? Have you experienced some of the negativity and deterioration spoken of in this chapter? Over the next thirty days, would

you be willing to ask God for a new way of seeing your partner? Try it!

3. Think about one of your partner's behaviors or traits that you find most irritating. Now sincerely ask God to show you the source of that behavior or personality trait. Perhaps it is a genetic disposition or a product of his or her childhood experience or even a result of some painful life experience. Let Him soften your heart and change your way of thinking about that source of irritation, maybe even giving you a spirit of gratitude toward your spouse. If you choose to share your answers with your spouse, (and I hope you will), remember to do so with loving tact for the feelings of your partner. St. Paul said, *"Speak the truth in love"* (Ephesians 4:15).

TRY THIS EXERCISE

Many, if not all, of the quirks of our partner's personality that bring out the worst in us are on a continuum that, if we took the time to consider, would be correlated to another feature of his/her personality we find attractive, or at least we once did. For instance, his seeming obsessive-compulsive way of doing things is on a continuum that includes his sense of responsibility and thoroughness. Her *"scattered-ness"* is on a continuum that includes her *spontaneity* and *enthusiasm* for life. You get the idea. Now take some time to consider your partner's traits in the light of such a view and see the positive expression of those traits. At the same time, think about how you can help to bring out the more positive expressions of those features.

CHAPTER TWELVE

The Holy Eucharist
From Home to Tabernacle

The worshiper is now prepared to receive the Blessed Sacrament. It is all but impossible to fully appreciate the sacrament of the Eucharist without at least a basic primer in the Old Testament. Or, to be more precise, we should say the Old Covenant. Recall those words of our Lord when He instituted the Eucharist that Thursday night before his arrest, *"This is my blood of the new covenant shed for many for the remission of sins."* To properly interpret salvation history, we must go back to the concept of covenant of which we spoke early on in this book. The new covenant does not erase these former covenants because God's Word remains true, even if not reflecting a fuller relationship.

There are multiple covenants found in the pages of the Old Testament, including the Adamic covenant with Adam, the Noahdic covenant with Noah, the Abrahamic covenant with

Abraham and the Davidic covenant with David. But the one that is central to our understanding of the Eucharistic meal is the Mosaic covenant with Moses on Mount Sinai. Having led the Hebrew slaves out of Egypt where they had become slaves over the previous 400 years since the death of their forefather Joseph, then leading them through the Red Sea and to the base of the mountain that was incensed with a cloud of God's glory, the great deliverer makes his way alone up the mountain where he is given the Law, known by scholars and theologians as the Decalogue—that is the Ten Commandments. But there is one more revelation he receives on the mountain in this incredible theophany. Moses is given entrance to the heavenly courts where he sees the Holy Tabernacle.

The writer of the book of Hebrews in the New Testament has one central objective in mind for his writing—to demonstrate without question that the covenant of Jesus Christ which He Himself made on our behalf with the Father to ensure our salvation for all eternity is far *superior* to any of the covenants that preceded it. He writes of the ministry of the High Priest saying, *"They worship in a copy and shadow of the heavenly sanctuary, as Moses was warned when he was about to erect the tabernacle. For he says, 'See that you make everything according to the pattern shown you on the mountain.' Now he has obtained so much more excellent a ministry as he is mediator of a better covenant, enacted on better promises"* (Hebrews 8:5-6). It is easy to see that the author of this ancient book is effectively laying out the case for the New Covenant in Jesus Christ to be ever so much more beautiful and complete than the former Mosaic covenant while at the same time not altogether different, just far better.

When he comes down the mountain, Moses will bring with him the architectural blueprint for the earthly tabernacle that would serve as the *portable* house of the Lord during the nomadic period of the people's wilderness wanderings until they would eventually come to the promised land of their father Abraham. The tabernacle was a spectacular edifice of beauty and untold symbolism. Although it would be referred to as a tent often in the pages of the Old Testament, it was anything but the kind of tent we might conceive in our 21st century minds. When constructed, the tabernacle took the shape of a rectangular box divided into two sections with curtains separating the two rooms. The outer premises around the tent would be considered holy ground and a proper reverence was required of the people drawing near.

In the Hebrew language, the comparative and superlative degree of magnitude is expressed through repetition. So, instead of saying that one area is holy and another is holier, the phrase in the Hebrew would be *holy* and *holy, holy*. To raise something to the second degree is to say that it is, in this case, holier than the holy place surrounding the tabernacle. The outer room of the tent was the *holy, holy place* where only the Levitical priests were allowed entrance to perform their ministerial functions. But the tabernacle was further divided so that beyond this holy place was the holiest place among the people and, for that matter, on the earth. It was the *holy, holy, holy place* where only the High Priest could enter and on only one day a year, the Day of Atonement (known in Hebrew as Yom Kippur), to make the annual sacrifices for himself and the people.

This sacred place of the Hebrew people contained the Ark of the Covenant—a box made by divine design with a lid that was pure gold in the shape of two angels whose outstretched wings hovered over the container. Inside, the covenant was placed on the tablets that Moses brought down from Mount Sinai; some of the manna the people ate in the wilderness and Aaron's rod that budded before the Pharaoh were kept inside as well. The Ark was decorated with the figures of two angels on the mercy seat. At the point where the angels' wings nearly touched was the Divine Light known as the *Shekinah*, signifying the very presence of Almighty God. Tradition held that the priests would tie a rope around the ankle of the High Priest on Yom Kippur before he would enter the Holy of Holies so that, in case he suffered death while in the presence of God, they could pull him out without exposing themselves to the sacred place.

This reverence for the Lord stands, sadly, in sharp contrast to the religious culture of most western Christians, who take a rather casual approach to God and to worship. At times, this irreverence may be a result of poor catechesis coupled with a naiveté about proper piety in the presence of God. At other times, it can be more of an intentional effort on the part of religious leaders and the faithful who want to bring the Almighty down to a more reachable place. And that is right and good, to an extent, for this is what God has done in the Incarnation of Jesus. In fact, the term used in John 1 when we read *"...and the Word became flesh and made his dwelling among us"*—the verb translated *made his dwelling* —is derived from the same word for *tabernacle*. So, an acceptable translation of the verse would be *"...and the Word became flesh and tabernacle'd among us"*. The typological significance is powerful, to say the least, given what we have described of the ancient tabernacle.

But this is not a book about liturgical form and practice. There are others who have written along these lines and challenge us greatly with our practices of worshipful observance. We have been exploring marriage. So, what has all this talk of tabernacles, holy places and postures of reverence to do with marriage? There are several directions we could turn as we explore the implications of the Eucharist for marriage. St. John Paul II gave to us a masterpiece on marital love in his *Theology of the Body*[17]. Authors and teachers like Michael Waldstein and Christopher West have provided us very comprehensible and practical ways to understand this theological work and apply it to our marriages. We could certainly advocate for the Eucharist as the sacrament to increase the faith and fidelity of the spouses. As we have said, the rituals of a marriage are a fundamental part of the marital dance that brings a spiritual rhythm into the home.

The focus I want to take is slightly different. Having described the ancient tabernacle, let's consider what that might mean for us in marriage. To do so, we must look at some New Testament passages. The first is in St. Paul's first letter to the Corinthians, a people who were surrounded with immorality of the worst kind. He admonishes them with this incredible reality—*"Do you not know that your body is a temple of the holy Spirit within you, whom you have from God, and that you are not your own?"* (I Corinthians 6:19). The apostle to the Gentiles is announcing to this non-Jewish audience, who would nonetheless have had some knowledge of how sacred the temple was to the Jewish people, that they themselves are dwelling-places for the Holy Spirit. Since the ascension of the Lord fifty days before the Day of Pentecost, when 3,000 were baptized into the church in Jerusalem at that first revival meeting, it was understood that the Holy Spirit is the Third Person of the Divinity whom Jesus would send for them to know, that God was still and always is present with them, even though He Himself would return to the Father.

There are three enormously powerful truths embedded in this announcement of St. Paul. First, he is boldly pronouncing that they are the new temple of God. Their fleshy bodies are the sacred dwelling-place of the Shekinah light—the Glory of the LORD. Can you imagine what these carnal-minded Corinthians would have thought when they heard or read these words? The Holy One of Israel who had led the ancient Hebrew people out of Egypt into the land of Canaan and driven out the pagan peoples, who dwelt in Solomon's Temple in the Holy of Holies, would now come to reside in their mortal bodies. That is an awe-some and awe-inspiring message that would change their entire understanding of both God and themselves.

Second, the apostle is using this great truth as the rationale for morally right behavior. He exhorts them, *"'Everything is lawful for me,'" but not everything is beneficial. "Everything is lawful for me,' but I will not let myself be dominated by anything. 'Food for the stomach and the stomach for food,' but God will do away with both the one and the other. The body, however, is not for immorality, but for the Lord, and the Lord is for the body; God raised the Lord and will also raise us by his power."* (1 Corinthians 6:12-15a). Read that line again and wrap your mind around the fact that you are bound up with Christ himself. Whether you accept it, feel it, or even believe it, Jesus Christ in bound up with you and you are bound up in Him. He writes further, *"Shall I then take Christ's members and make them the members of a prostitute? Of course not! [Or] do you not know that anyone who joins himself to a prostitute becomes one body with her? For 'the two,' it says, 'will become one flesh.' But whoever is joined to the Lord becomes one spirit with him."* (1 Corinthians 6:15b-17).

Paul has raised the stakes on what we do in these bodies of flesh to a level beyond comprehension. The sexual immorality that was so common among the community of Corinth must be understood by them as tantamount to what the Greeks did two centuries before Christ when the barbaric conquerors entered the Holy Temple and desecrated the altar with their pagan sacrifices, as if to join their ungodly heretical practices of so-called worship with the true worship of the Jewish people they had conquered. The inspired apostle teaches them that to practice immorality in the body when the Holy Spirit resides therein is to commit the same desecration.

And the third remarkable truth we can draw from this passage is that, if we are all made in the actual image of God our Creator, then we have a divine obligation to regard one another as such. Never is that statement truer than in the union of a husband and wife in marriage. How can we dare to treat anyone with disdain or wish ill upon them when that person is a *tabernacle of the Almighty*? The 20th century writer C.S. Lewis understood something of this when he wrote in his outstanding volume *The Weight of Glory*:

> "It is a serious thing to live in a society of possible gods and goddesses, to remember that the dullest most uninteresting person you can talk to may one day be a creature which, if you saw it now, you would be strongly tempted to worship, or else a horror and a corruption such as you now meet, if at all, only in a nightmare." [18]

Lewis' words convey the essential truth of the Pauline text about the sacredness of our bodies and, indeed, our very persons. He goes on to admonish us:

> "All day long we are, in some degree helping each other to one or the other of these destinations. It is in the light of these overwhelming possibilities, it is with the awe and the circumspection proper to them, that we should conduct all of our dealings with one another, all friendships, all loves, all play, all politics. There are no ordinary people. You have never talked to a mere mortal. Nations, cultures, arts, civilizations—these are mortal, and their life is to ours as the life of a gnat. But it is immortals whom we joke with, work with, marry, snub, and exploit—immortal horrors or everlasting splendors."

The strength of these words is surpassed only by the truth behind them, a truth that St. Paul desperately wants us to understand because, without such an understanding, we are tempted to profane the very ones the Lord has placed in our lives to honor. And again, this is never more applicable than in the covenant of the marriage relationship. The magnitude of his words is found in the reality that our attitude and behavior toward another person not only reflects our love for God and His creation, but also has an influence in the determination of where that person spends eternity. Now, if that does not impress upon you the significance of the way you relate to others, then your heart has hardened to a place where you may not be open to receive that same love from another and perhaps even God.

Particularizing this eternal principle to marriage should greatly impact the manner of our thoughts, conduct and every other aspect of our marriage relationships. This enterprise known as marriage is a holy endeavor, yes even as holy as the Eucharistic meal itself in which we participate every Mass. The sacramental reality of marriage can never be downplayed in our effort to understand or diminish its awesomeness. St. Paul verifies this teaching in his comments to the Ephesian church of the first century as he writes about marriage.

> "Husbands, love your wives, even as Christ loved the church and handed himself over for her to sanctify her, cleansing her by the bath of water with the word, that he might present to himself the church in splendor, without spot or wrinkle or any such thing, that she might be holy and without blemish. So [also] husbands should love their wives as their own bodies. He who loves his wife loves himself. For no one hates his own flesh but rather nourishes and cherishes it, even as Christ does the church, because we are members of his body. 'For this reason a man shall leave [his] father and [his mother and be joined to his wife, and the two shall become one flesh.' This is a great mystery, but I speak in reference to Christ and the church. In any case, each one of you should love his wife as himself, and the wife should respect her husband." (Ephesians 5:25-33)

Two imperatives stand out in this marital exhortation. The first is that our manner of love toward a spouse is to follow the pattern of Christ in His love for His own bride, the Church. This is no one other than sacrificial love that lays down its life for the sake of the beloved. That is a high calling, but we are empowered to accomplish it by the very grace that He provides in this sacrament. Peter began to understand this kind of love after his betrayal of his Lord in the garden on the night of Jesus' arrest. As we would expect, Peter was enormously distraught over his actions and humbled by his failure. In the last chapter of the Gospel of John we find an intriguing encounter between Jesus and Peter, where the Lord asks the disciple *"Do you love me?"* In fact, He asks him the same question three times, and Peter answers Him three times with the response *"I love you."* Some Scripture scholars say the repetition is due to the threefold denouncement of Jesus by Peter, hence a threefold restoration. I think the answer is found in the language behind the words. The Greek reveals that Jesus used the verb form of the word *agape* or *sacrificial love* when He asked Peter if he loved Him, while Peter responded with the verb form of the word *phileo* or *brotherly love* when he answered. Perhaps Peter, now humbled by his failure, had come to realize that brotherly love is indeed sacrificial.

Marriage requires sacrificial love beyond what we could ever have imagined when we uttered those vows of consecration to our spouse. Husbands and wives must live out *sacrificial brotherly love* daily if they are to have a lifelong friendship that reflects the friendship found in the Trinity. And I assure you that there will be countless opportunities to practice along the way.

The second imperative is that, in loving our partner in marriage, we *sanctify* our spouse. The term comes from the Greek word *hagias*, used in the Septuagint (Greek translation of the Old Testament) referring to the articles and vessels within the holy Tabernacle of worship. The rudimentary meaning is that they were to be *set apart* for a very special purpose and function. Much like you may have a special dining ware or silver ware that you reserve for only the most special of occasions, so it is with things of God. They are *set apart* for a sacred function and must never be used for commonplace activity or treated as anything less than sacred. This is the actual meaning of profanity—to take that which is holy and treat it as if it were common. How often does this characterize the behavior of a husband or wife toward the other?

And the final teaching that comes to us from this passage is that marriage is, as St. Paul says, *"...a great mystery..."* (v.32). The Greek term here is *musterion* – translated to the Latin term *sacramentum*, from which we get our English word *sacrament*. Even our Protestant brothers who may struggle with and even reject the theology of sacrament can do little to debate the truth herein that marriage is a tremendous mystery, defying the imagination of sacredness, an experiential spirituality warmed by the mystery of God. As a former minister in a non-denominational church, I very much appreciate how much of a difficulty this can be, to even use these kinds of terms like *sacrament*. It can conjure up the idea of some sort of man-made artificial religious practice that probably had its origins in the dark ages and had no compatibility with the Bible. As I began my studies in historical Christianity that eventually would lead me to the Catholic Church, my intrigue was heightened by the thought that I could truly encounter God in the flesh—that is, the flesh of the Eucharist. Oddly enough, it was my evangelical tradition that stressed so much the personal relationship with God through Jesus Christ that left me with much more of a platonic and academic knowledge of him. I hungered for more.

I remember coming across a book titled *Knowing God* by J.I. Packer[19] back in my seminary days. It struck a chord within me that maybe my hunger could be satisfied—that maybe a plan for realizing that personal relationship was available. I don't think I'm the only one who likes a plan. It's so much easier to follow a well laid out plan than it is to enter a mystery that defies description and eludes neatly organized *how-to* steps. Despite his impressive theological acumen, Packer came up short, offering yet another systematic theology—a good one at that, but not quite what I was expecting or needing. I wanted a person; he gave me another set of prescribed doctrinal truths. Please do not misunderstand me on this. I hope and strive to be orthodox in the best sense of the word—believing the right things. Yet there is a tension that too frequently exists in theology that posits an orthodox creed against an experiential spirituality into the mystery of God. Call me selfish but I want both. Furthermore, I think we are offered both in the historic Christianity found in the Catholic Church as expressed in its Holy Tradition and sacramental life.

Can you imagine a marriage where the two individuals are confined to a platonic and cerebral knowing of each other? Certainly, a cognitive knowledge of the other person is vital and foundational to the building of a strong marriage, yet the cognitive only whets the appetite for the experiential expression of the relationship. The ancients reflected this concept in their language for sexual intimacy, when they referred to the nuptial act as a *knowing* of the other. Marriage is not an intellectual dialogue in which the two partners exchange facts and information about and with each other. At least, that is not all it is. That kind of expression ushers them into a passion for the mystery. The Catholic understanding of that mystery is found in sacramental theology that tells us there is more than what can be seen, heard, sensed and even understood. Somewhere in the past four or five decades, I read or heard a story of two men having a conversation about their wives. The one asked the other, *"Do you love her?"* to which he replied, *"Yes, of course I love her!"* The first man asked a follow up question, *"Describe your wife to me."* The respondent began, *"My wife has brown hair, green eyes, is about five feet tall, is very caring and generous..."* He went on to give a physical and personality description of his wife that revealed his knowledge of his wife. As the verbal painting went on, the first man interrupted him and declared, *"You do not love your wife...for if you did you would not be able to describe her!"*

THE LITURGY OF MARRIAGE • 253

Now that story may strike us as a little extreme and even insensitive, but it does make a notable point. The person to whom you are married is more than the physical reality sitting before you. She is more than a set of descriptors, more than a personal history, more than a personality type. She is a mysterious child of our Creator God who mirrors His likeness in ways beyond words. This is the sacred inner sanctum I long for all married persons to believe and trust and pursue.

Virtually every day I step into my counseling practice office I will face at least one case where this painful condition is playing out, and let me quickly add that I could probably count on one hand the number of times I have encountered a couple who both wanted the divorce. With very few exceptions, it is one partner who has come to a place of hurt, despair, negativity and helplessness and has given up any hope of reconciliation, while the other partner is in a different place of hurt, despair, negativity and helplessness and yet clinging to a hope for reconciliation. Like a drowning victim desperately trying to hold onto another for dear life only to fuel the departure, so it is with one partner being left in the pitiful place of loneliness.

A Familiar Story

Mark and Beth were two months short of celebrating the 25th anniversary of their wedding and would soon pass from the parenting season into the proverbial empty nest season, during which they had once hoped to live out those dreams they shared at the beginning. Raising a family had taken its toll on the couple but, as is usually the case, very few outsiders would have ever guessed it. Their dual careers with very active lifestyles contributed to living in separate worlds. Their ships were passing but not connecting and it is uncertain whether their dreams had changed or just eroded. Women will normally *feel* the problems first. When Beth felt the pain in the marriage she would talk with a friend, buy another book, listen more intently to the weekly sermons, pray harder and sometimes pressure Mark to see a counselor.

Men normally dismiss the problems until they reach a crisis level. Now the crisis was upon him and it could not be ignored. His wife of twenty-five years was angry with him most of the time now and threw around the idea of separation and even divorce with an increasing regularity in their fights. This wasn't easy for her, as her Christian faith and family heritage would not allow her to even consider moving in that direction without sufficient cause. Yet, as dissatisfying as her marriage to Mark had been so much of the time, or at least it seemed to her that way now, she could find little moral grounds to justify the direction her pain was leading her.

She wasn't trying to be difficult and argumentative, but Mark couldn't do anything right in her eyes. Like most people in her emotional condition, her mental perspective was clouded with negativity allowing her only to see the bad and seemingly unable to give him the benefit of the doubt any longer. Immersed in pain her mind became absorbed with finding a way to feel better, recover hope for life, and make sense of her confusion. Psychology tells us there is so much more going on under the surface that gives explanation to the feelings, behaviors and symptoms visible on the surface. For Beth, what was occurring in her mind was a battle with one part sinking into despair, feeling trapped in the marriage, and another part trying desperately to build a case for ending the marriage.

Mark may not have been a model husband but he was faithful, so adultery was not an option for her to use as moral grounds. You see, even though the state may not require a basis or cause for divorce, most Christians still must have something substantial to which we can turn for justification of an action that is in stark contrast to our personal and religious values. It must make sense in some paradoxical way if we are going to go this far. He had never been physically abusive, so that charge was also empty. But she experienced emotional hurt from him on countless occasions and she'd read that this constitutes emotional abuse. The word *abuse* is a strong word that brings up terrible images for all of us. The *lawyer part* of Beth was latching onto this and became vigilant in search of any signs of emotional abuse, including his anger, yelling, cursing, threats, being out of control, name-calling, and any other irrational behavior.

The crazy-making part of all this for Mark was that his every attempt to hold back the tide of negativity and turn the flow toward reconciliation was met with resistance by Beth. He wanted to talk. She wanted space. He pursued. She withdrew. He pursued with pressure. She withdrew with vehemence. The dialogue goes something like this.

Mark: *"Can we talk?"*

Beth: *"I'm through talking!"*

Mark: *"What about counseling?"*

Beth: *"I wanted to do that five years ago. You're too late."*

Mark: *"How can you do this to our family?"*

Beth: *"I didn't do this...you did!"*

Mark: *"I love you. Let's work on our marriage. I don't want this"*

Beth: *"It's always about what you want, Mark! I'm tired of trying to make you happy!"*

Mark: *"Don't you see what this will do to the kids?"*

Beth: *"Stop trying to make me feel guilty! I'm through feeling to blame for the problems in this marriage."*

Mark's frustration mounts as he tries every futile attempt to convince his wife to give reconciliation a chance, but her sentiment toward him has deteriorated to the point that she has little left but anger for how he has failed her. Eventually he reaches a level of anger physiologists refer to as Diffuse Physiological Arousal (DPA also known as "Fight-or-Flight") and blurts out an expletive uncharacteristic of him.

Beth: *"And you call yourself a Christian?! This kind of abuse is exactly why I can no longer stay in this marriage!"*

She storms out in a fury of self-justifying anger, not quite able to recognize the role she played in contributing to that mutually frustrating conflict. He, on the other hand, feels bewildered, confused, and frustrated that his best efforts fall flat and even make the condition worse. Those feelings soon fuel his anxiety and depression as he faces the very outcome he has been trying desperately to avoid.

When a Marriage Dies

The death of a marriage affects all of us. Both partners will find their health at its worst during the demise with a suppressed immune system that leaves them at risk for an assortment of medical problems and can easily exacerbate any chronic conditions. They will easily meet the diagnostic criteria for an assortment of situational mood disturbances that could eventuate into more serious disorders. Medication and therapy can help reduce some of the symptomatic effects of marital distress and divorce but the condition is resistant to most interventions. Children will be affected without a doubt and regardless of age. Although most do adjust over time, they will bear the psychological marks throughout their lives often manifested in their own intimate relationships.

Many couples will try marriage counseling only to discover the powerlessness of the trained professional to soften a heart, change a potentially and likely distorted view of history, and bring about reconciliation. It does happen and I will work as hard as I can to bring about all those effects with every couple I encounter, yet too often the cancer has spread beyond the reach of treatment. The one who has come in hopes of a cure will stake everything on the process while the other has come with little more than a desire to convince the therapist and spouse that the condition is hopeless, not quite able to accept that he is driving that firmly held *prophecy* home. At the risk of being judgmental of one whose life has reached a seeming intolerable pain in the marriage, it is as though the one seeking the divorce needs to be able to say to herself, *"I tried everything, even marriage counseling. Nothing worked."*

Oh, the lengths our minds will go to ease the ambiguous tensions within our lives between our dreams and values and our disappointments and suffering. We all want relief and can fall into the temptation to pursue it when the pain exceeds our tolerance. The relief may come in the form of a divorce, but the reality of that post-divorce world carries its own challenges that may almost rise to the pre-divorce level. Alcohol and drugs, both legal and illegal, offer relief but at the expense of jobs, marriages, health, and so much more. Pornography provides momentary relief as it creates a fantasy in striking contrast to the reality of life, yet it will soon be replaced by a self-loathing shame. Affairs and new "lovers" offer relief from the struggle of a failing or failed marriage, but the discovery that every relationship brings its own set of problems and challenges can soon re-ignite the cancer.

Family and friends are drawn into the marital death as the exiting partner tries to justifiably explain the reason for the departure from the marriage and hopefully gain the much-needed support for future days. The rejected partner, on the other hand, will try to find the answers to turn back the tide that is taking his life away. It is all but impossible not to fall on one side or another whether by choice or default. We are all affected by the breakdown. If you are a strong proponent of marriage (which is not easy to find in this age) you will naturally want to confront the couple, particularly the spouse wanting the marriage to end, and offer them your words of encouragement and counsel in the hopes to save the marriage. One spouse will applaud your likely futile efforts and the other will feel judged and vilified. Even if your opinion is sought it may just be a test to determine where you stand on the divorce.

I want to bring an important clarification to this discussion of divorce. There is a great temptation to point the finger at the spouse who has decided to end the marriage as the culprit responsible for the breakdown. That is probably a terrible generalization to draw, as it overlooks the fact that he or she did not arrive at this place in a vacuum and without an historical context. Even as we talk about the deteriorated mindset or marital sentiment of the one partner that results in a type of revisionist history slanted horribly toward the negative, even this must be explored and given some understanding. Someone doesn't just wake up one morning and decide to think and feel poorly toward a spouse. It is a steady diet of negativity, neglect and hurt that leaves a partner vulnerable to the crisis of an affair or divorce. This part of the story can be easily overlooked in the wake of the conflict around a marital breakdown. It is certainly true that God hates divorce, but it is also true to say that God hates the things that bring about a divorce as well. So be gentle and grace-giving with anyone in the throes of the divorce tragedy.

A Good Gift

Any Catholic who has been practicing the faith for more than a few months has at some time in his life found himself taking the gift of the Eucharist for granted. It doesn't happen by design, nor is it necessarily a result of poor or weak faith. Just think back to the last gift you received. Perhaps it was an article of clothing for your birthday or that latest and greatest gadget from Apple or Microsoft. Regardless of the value, the cost, the giver, or the occasion we are all susceptible to the temptation to lose interest in the item or gesture. We valued it at the time it was given and received, but with the passage of time we have come to treat it as more ordinary than we did from the outset.

So it is with the Eucharist. Through prayerful study and deliberate intention, we receive our first Communion with a sense of awe and incredible gratitude. Then one day we awaken to realize that we have lost that zeal for the Mass and have become complacent in the exercise of our faith. Like a spiritual entropy, we feel our spirituality ebb and lose most of its flow. The hunger and thirst for a new taste nags at us. Have you ever had a family member or friend leave the Catholic Church for a Protestant ecclesial community? They probably told you that their needs were not being well met at the Mass or they found the music dull and the homily boring or perhaps that they never found a sense of fellowship in the Church. Then came an exposure to something altogether different and experientially exciting. Their senses came alive with the setting, the music, the ambiance, the teaching and the community. And so, they left and never came back...that is, unless they discovered the void outside the Catholic Church when the Eucharist is not present.

Many "cradle Catholics" have had their faith challenged by an enthusiastic evangelical Protestant who introduced them to one of their worship services. The difference is quite evident from the moment you enter the place. From the coffee bar with qualified barista in the lobby to the theatre seating to the professional praise music band to the strong preaching from the young man in jeans and an open-neck casual shirt, it will strike you that this is a well-polished event. If you want to be inspired and have a wonderful experience of emotional uplifting, then a typical evangelical worship service will more than satisfy. These are my roots, so I have a strong affinity for the phenomena and frankly miss the opportunity to enter the preaching and teaching role with a congregation of worshipers anxious to hear the Word of God and receive instruction.

What is the problem? Why all the fuss with tradition, liturgy, incense, standing, kneeling, genuflecting and all the rituals that accompany sacramental faith practice? At the risk of over-simplification, I would say that the fundamental difference in Protestant and Catholic worship lies not in the rituals, the prayers, the incense or any of the other seemingly incidental elements (though, of course, a proper understanding of liturgy would recognize that none of the elements are ever incidental). The core distinctive of sacramental worship is *sacrifice*. Worship is not just singing or praying or fellowshipping or studying the Word. It is stepping into the sacrificial offering of our Lord Jesus Christ. This is H*is* liturgy; the work performed by our Lord on behalf of the global community. This is the sacrifice of the Mass! To say more would be both repetitive and perhaps critical, so let me just encourage you to think about these matters, talk with a Catholic priest, read a book by a Catholic theologian, or even step foot into the doors of a Catholic Church and the experience of the Mass. It is heavenly if you give yourself to what is taking place!

Marital Love is Sacrificial

The Beatles may have been right when they declared and set to unforgettable music the fundamental truth in their song title—*All You Need Is Love*. The statement is sound. The definition is lacking. How do we define love? Friendship is love of course. Few would deny that sharing and giving is part of love. But is that a complete definition of love? Our faith informs us that the only love that will sustain a couple through the highs and lows of marriage will be *sacrificial* in its essential nature. How else could a woman endure the emotional wounding of a career-centered husband who too often neglects her and their children in deference to his vocational pursuits? How else could an introverted husband patiently tolerate his wife's endless social engagements? How else could a couple remain married when they have failed each other so much and hurt each other so deeply? How else could two people continue to value each other for their unique glory spoken of by C.S. Lewis? The answer—*Sacrificial Love!*

If I had a time machine, I am confident that I could bring healing to every marriage. I would conduct two interventions with that time machine. First, I would ask the couple to step into the machine and then set the dial to the year the couple met. They would re-experience those courting days of their relationship. Given that no one has yet found the key to the time-escaping invention, I will try to do this with the couple by asking them to share their story with me while I listen intently, questioning curiously every detail along the way in my effort to re-kindle some of those early emotional memories deeply hidden beneath the pain that brought to me in the first place. The second intervention I would perform with the time machine would be to take them into their eternal future. This I would do to give them that glimpse into their glorified states where they can then see each other as the persons God created them to be. I am altogether certain they would fall into the glory of divine sacrificial love for each other!

If only that scientific genius would come along to put the mathematical pieces together and engineer the time-defying device that will heal all our marriages. Do not despair, for God has in fact and truth given us that timeless experience in the holy Mass. The sacrifice of the Mass affords us the awesome opportunity to see God in His trinitarian holiness of sacrificial love. It also affords us the sacramental mirror through which we can see ourselves and be brought to our knees in contrite worship. And it affords us the sacramental portal through which we can see our spouse for the person God created him or her to be. The inescapable outcome of this sacrificial journey is love!

What did people do before the invention of counseling, therapy, psychotherapy? How did they ever find emotional healing? How did they re-orient themselves to a good way of living when they lost their way? How did they reconcile from their marital failings? My educated guess would be through the sacraments and especially the Mass. It is not just the sacrament of the Anointing of the Sick that brings healing, although it is the clearest demonstration of such. Each of the seven has a health-giving dimension that deserves consideration and appreciation. But we must have a right understanding of healing before we will ever come to that place.

Say the word *healing* and listen to the reactions. To the boy who just broke his arm falling off his bike, healing comes in terms of the elimination of pain, removal of the cast, and a return to full capacity to ride again. Not too different from the response any of us have when our bodies break. To the woman in lonely tears who has just buried her husband of sixty-three years, healing will mean nothing less than resurrection. To the mentally ill, healing will mean hope. It means something different to all of us. The word healing comes to us from the Old English *haelan*, a derivative from Proto-Germanic *hailjan*, meaning *"to make whole"*. This is a very powerful realization for us. If anything is evident from the Edenic fall it is that confounding brokenness is an inevitable result of sin. Living outside the *Garden*, we are all exposed to exponential levels of painful brokenness in our worlds of the physical, the emotional, the psychological, and the interpersonal. Marriage, regardless how *edenic* it may be at its inception, will sadly succumb to that epidemic brokenness. We ought not be surprised when it appears.

Some will take this pain-filled marital brokenness as indication that we made a poor choice in our selection of a mate. Nothing could be further from the truth. It has been said —*"Success in marriage is much more than finding the right person...it's a matter of being the right person."* Good words worth keeping in mind when we fall into that negative marital sentiment that views our spouse as the *wrong person* for us. We are all affected daily by the brokenness of humanity. Marriage is no exception. The healing we need is a recovery of wholeness made possible through our union with Christ.

Bringing It Home

In this litigious world where people sue at the drop of a hat, the concept of *covenant* is a fresh idea, even if it is an age-old practice that comes to us from antiquity itself. Recognizing the Eucharist as a culmination of over 2000 years of purposeful salvation history is staggering. We are dining in covenantal meal with Abraham, Moses and David. We are sharing communion with Peter, James and John. We are in prayer with Origen, Cyril, Therese and Augustine. We celebrate Mass with John of the Cross, Thomas Aquinas and Francis. This is what liturgy gives us—a portal into eternity!

THE HOLY EUCHARIST

1. There are so many incredible stories given to us in Holy Scripture of God's encounter with man. As you reflect on Abraham, Moses, Ruth, David, Elijah, Isaiah, Ezekiel, Mary, or any of the great men and women of the Bible, which one stands out to you? Why?

2. Imagine you are the High Priest of the people of Israel in the days of the Tabernacle when the people traveled about like a nomadic tribe. It is now that one day of the year

known as the Day of Atonement and you awaken in the morning to realize this is the day you will enter the sacred presence of Yahweh to make sacrifice for your sins and the sins of the entire people of Israel. How do you feel? What are you thinking? Describe the experience of anticipation. Does this realization motivate you to contrition for your own sins, perhaps even receiving the Sacrament of Reconciliation before you receive the Holy Eucharist?

3. Now consider that each time you enter the Church to celebrate the Holy Mass you are participating in a sacred act every bit as holy as the one just described for the High Priest. Now how do you feel? What are you thinking? Describe the experience of anticipation of not only being before your Holy Lord God, but even receiving Him into your body and soul in such a manner that you become yourself the tabernacle of God. Soak it in!

TRY THIS EXERCISE

For this exercise, you will write your spouse a very special personal letter from your heart. Tell your partner what you see in him/her that reflects a unique beauty that speaks of God's design. Describe in detail some of your spouse's qualities and express how grateful you are for having been on the receiving end of those God-given charisms. Give words to the awe you feel as you contemplate the person of your spouse and how God has fashioned him/her as the individual he/she is. Let the words flow and share them in a spirit of gratitude for the gift He has given you in your marriage relationship.

CHAPTER THIRTEEN

The Concluding Rites
Taking His Sacred Presence Home and Into the World

O ne of the best compliments I have ever received is when someone says of me, *"He's a family man."* They are recognizing the value I place on my marriage and family and I want very much for the world to see it lived out in my life. Well we might say of our Lord and Creator, *"He's a family God."* God loves children. It comes as no surprise that the Church's view of marriage is consistent with the teaching of the Scripture about divorce—that is, to bring children into the world and ultimately populate heaven. Recall that we heard the prophet Malachi declare God's hatred of divorce because it hinders His desire for *"godly offspring"* (Malachi 2:15-16). In his essential nature God is *Father, Son and Holy Spirit*—family! Relationship is at the heart of our Creator and it is a holy love that breathes throughout His familial essence. Quite naturally

271

He would want to bring more children into that family of love. Theologians speak of the *economy of salvation*, drawing from the Greek word *oikonomos*, meaning "household," as they attempt to help us understand the entirety of salvation history as God's effort to restore mankind to His household, His family.

The teachings of the Catholic Church are neither arbitrary nor artificial, rather flowing from the eternal, immutable (non-changing) nature of God Himself. Why does the Church not allow for divorce? Because divine (sacramental) oneness can never be broken, just as the Trinity can never be broken. Why does the Church not allow for sex outside of marriage? Because it rejects the purpose of marriage to bring life into the family. Why does the Church forbid contraception? Because it denies fruitfulness in the marriage. Why does the Church stand boldly against abortion? Because it kills the child whom God has brought to life. Why does the Church reject any definition of marriage that is not an exclusive union between a man and a woman? Because it does not permit life. I will let the articulate theologians make the case far more eloquently than I could ever do, but we must never assume these teachings and practices to be without substance.

God loves children. Jesus invited the little ones to come to him. As a grandfather of nine beautiful ones, now I can better understand this love. We are called to populate heaven and our present world is doing it poorly, choosing instead the comforts afforded a marriage without children. Worldly values that extol the individual while discounting family are tempting when posited against the challenges of child-rearing, not to mention the costs. Experts are correct in saying that parenthood will push us to maturity faster than almost anything else in this world, testing our patience and taxing our resources. From the moment that infant takes its first breath in this world, her father and mother will be forever changed. Our society tells us to take a lesser value of these things and to pursue the temporal happiness that comes at the price of more work, more play and more self-centeredness. But all of this presumes the world in which we live is all there is and ever will be. If that were true then such selfish ambition might be warranted, or at least understood. It is eternity that beckons us to look at all of this differently. The Creator has a different plan than the world around us; a plan to bring as many people into his family to live with him eternally as possible. We are part of that plan.

Our work as Christians has become more difficult and even more necessary considering the sociological climate of the day. The world needs to see an alternative version of marriage. Holy matrimony requires definition and distinction in this culture. Couples have discovered that this form of godly marriage provides ultimate meaning and purpose to their relationship even during the change, difficulty and suffering which accompany any marriage. The Mass asks us to leave the liturgy and to enter the world prepared to share His love. To draw upon the rubric of the Mass' liturgy to explore marriage in this book, we are reminded of the need to enter the world from the sacramental contexts of our marriages and to reflect the glory of God evident in the matrimonial sacrament. Evangelicals have a phrase they are fond of using—*You may be the only Bible anyone ever reads.* The point is clearly to emphasize how critical it is that our lives are consistent with the teachings of Scripture so as not to turn anyone away from Christ through a hypocritical lifestyle. With a bit of modification, we are admonishing that the sacrament of marriage may be the only reflection of God's glory people witness. This means that, as married couples, we have both a privilege and a responsibility to live out our marital relationships in such a way that others can see God's glory through us.

All of this necessitates that we ask ourselves some difficult but challenging questions:

- **Do others see mutual sacrifice in your marriage?**
- **Are you exemplifying trinitarian love?**
- **Would it be recognizable that you both love God above all else?**
- **Does faith take priority over lesser passions?**
- **Is your lifestyle consistent with your profession of faith?**

Not easy questions for any of us and I have yet to see a perfect marriage. What I have seen are couples who found their way to a relationship much closer to this kind of godly love, usually through problems, challenges, and even failure. Couples who discovered that this form of godly marriage provides ultimate meaning and purpose to the relationship even amid change and difficulty and suffering, which are guaranteed realities in this world.

We take those vows at the marriage ceremony and repeat those words, *"...for better or for worse"* but few of us think that the "worse" will ever happen. Underlying our excitement is the naïve assumption that we will have a marriage different from all others—one characterized by the *better*, the *richer*, and the *health*. I am not saying we should be pessimistic about our futures, but we must be prepared for the *worse*, the *poorer*, and the *sickness*. How else will a marriage survive all we will face in the years to come? Can anything but a sacramental bond endure the fiery tests of this world and come out as the refined gold of godliness? This is a great mystery according to the words of St. Paul, but that mysterious wonder is made possible through the grace given us as we offer our marriage up to the Lord on the altar of sacrificial faith only to receive it back as the good gift that it is.

I must admit I'm a sucker for a good romance. It's a good thing because otherwise my wife and I might not be able to find a movie we could both watch and enjoy. And who writes a better romance novel than Nicholas Sparks? With predictable narrative, he tells story after story of couples' journeys of love.

Unfortunately, like most of the novels and films of our day, the love is much more erotic and based more on temporal values that may succumb to the fires of time. Just this morning, I was kneeling at my pew having just received the body and blood of our Lord in the Eucharist, and I observed the husband and wife in front of me kneeling together with their arms intertwined. In a beautiful fashion, they grasped each other's hands as if to exemplify in their touch the blessing they had received only moments earlier. This is a portrait of sacred love. We are inspired when we hear these stories of love touching something deeply right within us. St. John Paul II may have been referring to this when he wrote in *Theology of the Body* of the "echo of innocence."

My wife and I are right now on a sojourn throughout Italy. It is a wonderful experience we have been long anticipating. Two days ago, we were in Verona where Shakespeare's famous Romeo & Juliet was said to have taken place. Along with countless hundreds, we made our way into the small courtyard where we could look up and see the famous balcony Romeo climbed to deliver his red rose and say those romantic words to his love. Just because we chose not to push our way through the crowds and pay the exorbitant price to have your picture taken as you kiss on the balcony does not mean that we are not a romantic couple who still are drawn to the beauty of a good love story. Emotions are a part of the human personality meant to be enjoyed. It is only when they serve as the foundation for the relationship that it becomes a problem. One of my professors liked to say that emotions are the *fruit of the relationship, not the root.*

We can all be easily lured into an elusive search for the emotional source of happiness. The search becomes addictive precisely because its felt experience followed by the predictable let down fuels the desire for more. Unfortunately, a spouse will not be able to provide all the stimulation desired by the other spouse on this quest and those ups and downs of marriage will disappoint the one not ready for the mutual love of a mature relationship. Don't require of your wife that she be a fictitious *Juliet* who exists only in the imagination of young lovers. Let your husband be the man he is and not the *Romeo* you may desire him to be. Let reality be enough!

And so, we come to the end of this liturgical journey of marriage. Through these pages, we have navigated through some of the rudiments of a good relationship to draw from our incredible Christian faith as well as the findings of science. I hope you will be able to apply what you have read and weave these principles and ideas into the fabric of your marriage. Let your love shine in this dark world to reflect the incomparable glory of our God and Creator, the One who gave us marriage, sanctifies marriage, and gives the grace to live faithfully in marriage.

Bringing It Home

The government may change its definition of marriage but that in no way alters God's design for this sacred institution. Secular cultures are rarely friendly to marriage and family. Today's culture assaults people of Christian faith and then denies us the right to defend ourselves. We are left to enter the sufferings of Jesus Christ and bear our crosses with trust in the One who first died for us that we might live forever with Him. Marriage is a taste of that heavenly home. Never let the world rob you of the exquisite joy of marital love that can lift you to the hope of an Eden in glory where we will celebrate the great marriage feast of the Lamb and enjoy for eternity the love of the Father, Son and Holy Spirit!

THE CONCLUDING RITES: TAKING HIS SACRED PRESENCE HOME AND INTO THE WORLD

1. Have you experienced challenges to your view of marriage? What has been your response? In thinking about it now, would you change the way you responded to those who dispute our Christian understanding of marriage?

2. When you enter the sacred mysteries of the Mass, do you do so with your spouse at your side and in your mind and

heart? How can you deepen your marital love through the way you celebrate the Eucharist?

3. Ask God to show you another couple who need your prayers. Commit to praying for that couple daily for the next nine days, asking the Lord to open their hearts to receive what He has in store for them.

TRY THIS EXERCISE

When couples are ready to conclude their work with me as their marriage counselor, I try to prepare them for the natural tendency for things to revert to their original state as they stop exploring their marriage relationship. I then encourage them to think through some of the ways they will prevent that backward slide and maintain the progress they have made. I like to call this a *Marriage Maintenance Plan*. Take some time to develop your own plan for how you will give ongoing attention to your marriage relationship and push back on the tide of time that can erode the growth you have made as you worked through this book. Discover for yourselves a new *liturgy for your marriage*.

Bibliography

Brueggemann, Walter. (2007). *Praying the Psalms: engaging scripture and the life of the spirit.* Eugene: Cascade Books.

Lewis, C. S. (1952). Mere Christianity: A revised and enlarged edition, with a new introduction, of the three books The case for Christianity, Christian behavior, and Beyond personality. New York: Macmillan.

Lewis, C. S. (1949). *The Weight of Glory: And Other Addresses.* New York: HarperCollins.

Omartian, S. (2014). *The Power of a Praying Husband.* Irvine, CA: Harvest House Publishers.

Omartian, S. (2014). *The Power of a Praying Wife.* Irvine, CA: Harvest House Publishers.

Packer, J. I. (1973). *Knowing God.* Downers Grove: Intervarsity Press.

Pope Francis, *Amoris Laetitia* [Post-Synodal Apostolic Exhortation of the Holy Father Francis to Bishops, Priests and Deacons, Consecrated Persons, Christian Married Couples and all the Lay Faithful on Love in the Family, released April 8, 2016.

Pope John Paul II, *The Theology of the Body according to John Paul II: Human Love in the Divine Plan*. Boston: Daughters of St. Paul, 1997.

Pope Paul VI, *Gaudium Et Spes [Pastoral Constitution on the Church in the Modern World]*, Washington: United States Catholic Conference, 1965.

Weiss, R.L., & Heyman, R.E. (1997). *Marital Interaction*. In W. Halford and H. Markman (Eds.), *Clinical handbook of marriage and marital interaction*. New York: Wiley.

Notes

[1] Pope Paul VI, Gaudium Et Spes *[Pastoral Constitution on the Church in the Modern World]*, Washington: United States Catholic Conference, 1965.

[2] Copyright © 1994, United States Catholic Conference, Inc. -- Libreria Editrice Vaticana. Used with Permission.

[3] Lewis, C. S. (1952). *Mere Christianity: A revised and enlarged edition, with a new introduction, of the three books The case for Christianity, Christian behavior, and Beyond personality.* New York: Macmillan.

[4] John Paul II, *The Theology of the Body according to John Paul II: Human Love in the Divine Plan.* Boston: Daughters of St. Paul, 1997.

[5] Copyright © 1987 Birdwing Music (ASCAP) Sparrow Song (BMI) Greg Nelson Music (BMI) Universal Music - Brentwood Benson Songs (BMI) (adm. at CapitolCMGPublishing.com) All rights reserved. Used by permission. International Copyright Secured. All Rights Reserved. Used by Permission.

[6] Copyright © 1988 Universal Music - Brentwood Benson Publ. (ASCAP) (adm. at CapitolCMGPublishing.com) All rights

[7] Brueggemann, Walter. (2007). *Praying the Psalms: engaging scripture and the life of the spirit.* Eugene: Cascade Books.

[8]http://www.haggadot.com/clip/dayenu-english-hebrew-and-transliteration

[9]http://www.seattlepi.com/news/article/Billy-Graham-Bible-is-God-s-love-letter-to-us-1246557.php

[10] Pope Francis, *Amoris Laetitia* [Post-Synodal Apostolic Exhortation of the Holy Father Francis to Bishops, Priests and Deacons, Consecrated Persons, Christian Married Couples and all the Lay Faithful on Love in the Family, released April 8, 2016.

[12]   http://www.usccb.org/beliefs-and-teachings/what-we-believe/

[13] Koenig, H. http://www.spiritualityandhealth.duke.edu/

[14] Copyright © 2000-2013 by Dr. John M. Gottman and Dr. Julie Schwartz Gottman. Distrubuted under license by The Gottman Institute, Inc.

[15] Books by Stormie Omartian can be found on her website - https://www.stormieomartian.com.

[16] Weiss, R.L., & Heyman, R.E. (1997). *Marital Interaction*. In W. Halford and H. Markman (Eds.), *Clinical handbook of marriage and marital interaction*. New York: Wiley.

[17] John Paul II, *The Theology of the Body according to John Paul II: Human Love in the Divine Plan*. Boston: Daughters of St. Paul, 1997.

[18] Lewis, C. S. (1949). *The Weight of Glory: And Other Addresses*. New York: HarperCollins.

[19] Packer, J. I. (1973). *Knowing God*. Downers Grove: Intervarsity Press.

Tim & Margie Heck

Dr. Timothy Heck is a licensed marriage and family therapist in Indianapolis, Indiana with Family Counseling Associates, a group mental health practice founded by Tim in 1993 (FCAHelp.com). A formerly ordained Protestant Pastor Tim and his wife, Margie, entered the Catholic Church in 2003 after several years of diligent study, regular dialogue and arduous prayer. They enjoy opportunities to share their faith-filled story and encourage others in their journeys of faith. Tim and Margie have been blessed with five children and ten grandchildren, the loves of their lives. They are available for talks, presentations, parish missions, and retreats and can be reached at:

www.LiturgyofMarriage.com

info@liturgyofmarriage.com

CPSIA information can be obtained
at www.ICGtesting.com
Printed in the USA
BVOW03s0156180817
492237BV00004B/185/P